Happy while Hermitting Handbook
A Guide for Your Isolation

Samantha Varnerin

ISBN-13: 9798693090729

Cover design by: Lucy Luu
Printed in the United States of America

Contents

If Nothing Else, Read The Next Page of this Book

And also join our Facebook Group: facebook.com/groups/samsbook

I wrote this book with the plan to help you when you're in isolation. However, I write this while looking at several books on my own shelf that I never read all the way through. You may fully intend to read this book cover to cover now. You might even have pretty pens to use with this book or a separate journal. If you, like me, tend to do this and still end up not finishing partway through this page is for you. If you finish this page, put this book down, and never open it again, you've already gleaned more from this book than before you opened it.

This entire book, summarized in one sentence, can be boiled down to this:

Stop reacting automatically to the things in your life and start responding intentionally instead.

Look, you might be alone right now, but that doesn't mean you have to be lonely. In fact, this is a really good opportunity to shake things up and change your life in isolation and outside of it. You can create more meaningful connections with your friends even from afar. You can stop being afraid of being alone with your thoughts and feel love from yourself. You can form healthier habits that make your life more fulfilling. You can communicate better with the people around you and understand the people you love better in the moments when you normally would lash out on them. You can question why you believe the things you do, create lasting change in the world, and live your life with more empathy and love for other people that you haven't even met yet. So much is possible simply by responding intentionally instead of reacting automatically. The rest of this book is about all of these particular applications, and guides you in doing them better.

I personally found specific areas of responding intentionally in your life vital for my own sense of self when I was injured at the end of January 2019. That year was supposed to be my best year yet, but after visiting a trampoline park and tearing my ACL I was put three months behind that schedule. I couldn't work, I couldn't drive, and I couldn't even stand long enough to feed myself some days. It got to the point where I moved back in with my parents from my apartment outside of Boston to their new house they recently bought in Cape Cod while I recovered from my injury and surgery. At age 28, I was convinced my life was never going to be the same.

When I came back to Boston in April 2019, I realized my life wasn't ever going to be the same, but not for the reasons I thought. My life felt more wealthy, fulfilling, empowering, and connected than I had before my injury. It wasn't always easy to live with my parents and deal with my ACL injury far away from my friends and loving boyfriend. That said, my period in isolation with my parents was exactly what I needed to make a massive improvement in so many areas of my life. There's no way I would have had the same amazing changes in my life had I simply kept going at the unsustainable pace I was going pre-injury.

In March of 2020, the country closed down in order to fight COVID-19. During my long drive to see the last client I'd see just before I shutdown, it hit me that everyone was about to experience isolation like I had the year before. More worrisome to me was the fact that many might not be able to grow in their environments like I had the privilege to the previous year. I wanted to help, so I intentionally began to write this book. I hope you respond to these lessons intentionally as well.

Introduction:

Let's Accept That This Sucks. (But We're Going To Be Okay Too.)

I thought my life was pretty good in January 2019. I was gaining a strong and reputable following in my industry. I was working a lot but I was getting by financially just fine. My Inner Critic was vocal with me but I wasn't letting her stop me too much. My friends were organizing chill house events to hang out all the time and my boyfriend and I were open with our feelings. Everyone seemed accepting of me expressing myself. I was confident in my moral compass and what I believed in. At 28 years old, I felt like my life was beginning to pull away from the typical chaos my friends and I had experienced constantly in our early 20's. I felt like this was epitome of my life, and my connection with myself and others was as strong as it would ever be. However, going into a trampoline park with my boyfriend on a frigid early afternoon in January quickly proved to me that I couldn't have been more wrong.

We removed our sneakers in the open lobby and put them in a blue locker on the entrance wall. Everyone had to take their shoes off before entering the trampoline area. I remember suggesting to my boyfriend, Noah, that we should stretch so we wouldn't pull anything while jumping around.

"Good idea," Noah said. He leaned over to his straightened leg to reach for his ankle. I did the same, mirroring his stretching routine.

I stood up to hold my bent leg by the ankle behind my back, and something caught my eye. I didn't notice the sign for long-term passes near the park entrance. The sign said that you could get a monthly pass to the park for a decent price. *Maybe if today goes well, I'll get a monthly pass and come here more often to work out*, I thought to myself. It seemed like a fun way to get some exercise. The last time I had come here was fun, but I remembered getting out of breath within a couple minutes. As I leaned forward and felt my stomach tighten around the waistband of my yoga pants a little more, I thought to myself that the monthly pass might not be a bad idea to just get now and use it later. I shook my head, thinking I would wait and see how today goes.

We walked over to the foam mats leading to the trampolines. A young teenage girl around 15 years old who looked like she would rather be anywhere else but there very quickly and very monotonously rattled off three main safety rules to remember. We nodded and said "Okay" to her safety rules. She then waved us towards the trampolines behind her, many of which already had children and young teenagers bouncing on them.

Noah and I wandered to the back of the trampoline park to find some long rows of trampolines, all connected by foam pads between them, essentially making one giant trampoline. On the back row were more trampolines angled upwards against the walls. Before we made our way over to them, we saw other teenagers in the opposite corner bouncing on their trampolines, occasionally bouncing off of the vertically upwards ones and landing squarely on their horizontal trampolines. I could see Noah getting a little excited watching them. He had always loved doing intricate physical activities like Blues dancing and Capoeira, which was exactly why I brought him there for our date.

Noah took the lead getting into the Square setup of trampolines by bouncing on the First Trampoline once and making his landing onto the trampoline next to it, slowly bouncing over to the trampolines by the back wall. I followed, feeling myself sink into the first trampoline's center and kicking straight up. I realized I would need to bounce with my body slightly forward in order to bounce to the back corner with Noah. As I started falling back down, I bent my legs for another kick and leaned slightly forward. This time, the arc for my bounce would move towards the next trampoline. As I started falling, I noticed I wouldn't make the next trampoline. Instead, I landed on the foam frame connecting the two.

As I landed, I felt my heels dig into the foam frame and felt a hard metal underneath it. Rather than have a soft landing like I expected, I felt the momentum come to a sudden stop at my feet. The impact felt like it vibrated up my entire body to completely freeze me. It felt disorienting for a few seconds, but I quickly regained my composure. I didn't want to feel like that again, that's for sure. *Maybe I'll just walk over to the back trampolines for now*, I thought.

When I finally reached the corner where Noah was, I started bouncing as high as I could on the trampoline next to him. Once I got a good feel for when the top of my bounce would be, I projected myself about nine feet above the trampoline and kicked my legs in the air softly, trying to mimic a pose I saw in Mulan at some point.

I grinned at Noah, and he gave me a toothless smile back. His bounces on his trampoline were soft and only projected him about three or four feet above the trampoline. I was wondering if he was actually enjoying himself. Coming here was my idea, but he had said days before that he wanted to do something different than just sitting at home together. This was one of the first things I thought of, so I was hoping he would enjoy himself a little more. I was trying to think of different ways to make this more fun for us when I saw two teenagers bouncing off their butt and then back on their feet. *That looks fun! Let's try that,* I thought. After bouncing high, I curled up and assumed a cannonball position. I felt my butt and my back make contact with the trampoline and felt it catapult me back up. I opened up my Cannonball and began falling, bouncing back onto my feet and laughing the whole way down.

I turned to Noah to see how he was doing. He was bouncing about the same height as he was before, but this time he started bouncing off of the vertical trampolines. Every time he did it, he smiled a little bit more for a moment. I looked around at kids on trampolines nearby beginning to do similar tricks off of the vertical trampolines. I was a little hesitant to try since I had never done it before. Noah, however, was making it look pretty easy.

I was still bouncing high and wondering if bouncing off the vertical trampolines was something I should try. Everyone else seemed to be having a lot of fun trying it out, and even though it looked a little scary, it also seemed easy to do. Mid-bounce, I decided to go for it.

That was literally the worst possible time I could have gone for it. Everyone else made it look so easy and fun. Unfortunately for me, my mind decided to go for it after I had already jumped instead of before like everyone else, so my timing was off. Instead of landing back on the horizontal trampoline, I ended up sliding down the vertical one and not making it to the horizontal one at all. I began panicking as I realized I would probably fall on the outer foam frame instead of the trampoline. My mind flashed to that awful vibrating feeling I felt earlier. I braced myself and tried to get my feet onto that frame.

As quickly as I slid down with my body against the vertical trampoline, I straightened my legs and bared my heels, bracing for the impact. I knew this was going to hurt no matter how I landed on this foam frame with hard metal underneath it. I felt my feet make contact with the frame and felt my upper body waver and struggle to find balance. With my legs still straight upon landing, I felt the vibration from earlier spread from my heels up to my hips as I felt disoriented and lost balance for a split second after making contact. It was then that I heard a deafening pop from my left knee.

I shifted my weight onto my left leg and felt excruciating pain. It felt concentrated in my knee, a place I never felt pain before. Normally when I got injured I would feel it in my ankles or my hamstrings. But as I attempted to put weight on my left leg, the only place I felt the horrible pain was in my knee. My calf spasmed and cramped, too weak to bear the weight of my entire body without my knee helping. I tried to squat or bend the knee but it refused to and was already beginning to swell.

Between this pop and this 2 second realization, I panicked. *I'm injured,* I realized. *I'm hurt. Not just a little either… this feels really bad.* I felt the sharp pains shoot through my knee again. *Ow! I can't just walk this off. This is really serious. I can't even put weight on it without it hurting.* I fell off the foam frame with my back landing on my trampoline, rolling to my side so I could clutch my throbbing and swelling knee.

Despite what sounded to me like a loud pop and this two second internal dramatic dialogue on my pain, Noah's back was to me and still bouncing, completely oblivious to what just happened and how much pain I was in. I felt bad. We hadn't even been on the trampolines for ten minutes of our hour long passes. *I guess we're not getting that monthly membership now*, I thought bitterly to myself. I began to sob and called out to him. "Noah. Noah!" I croaked out, pleading for his attention. Could he even hear me?

He finally turned mid bounce and saw me on the ground. His satisfied smile dropped quickly and turned into wide eyed horror as he saw me laying flat on the trampoline next to him, tears spilling out of my eyes. "Sam!" He exclaimed. He slowed his bouncing and stepped gently onto the foam frame that destroyed my knee. "What happened?"

"Get the staff and help me! I can't stand up on my own."

I never really had any serious injuries before that point. Sure, I'd pulled hamstrings or sprained ankles and even fractured my jaw at one point, but it was never anything really serious. I was convinced that this injury would take no more than a month or two before I was back to my regularly able-bodied self. However, it wasn't until three weeks into my injury that I found out I completely tore my ACL. I would need surgery to replace my ACL and a full year to do any activity beyond walking. In the meantime, I would need focused support and recovery for a month before surgery and for two to five months after surgery.

Focused support and effort weren't things I could easily do in my very-inaccessible apartment in Boston. I could barely make it into the kitchen without falling, yet alone drive to the grocery store. While I resisted the idea of leaving my apartment in Boston and getting more help recovering from my injury, it was clear within the first week of not being able to walk that I was going to be recovering for at least a few weeks, if not months. I needed family support to get better, and I'm thankful to be privileged enough that my family could have their injured adult daughter stay in their home during this difficult time. However, my parents had moved out of our hometown the year before and now lived in Cape Cod, an area that's known for not being super busy or happening outside of the summer season. Staying with my parents in January didn't just mean I would isolate away from everything and everyone I was familiar with. It also meant I would focus on my physical recovery with family members I hadn't lived with for nearly ten years in a town I was unfamiliar with.

I thought this time away was going to ruin my life. To be gone and move my focus at such an essential time in my career, my relationship, and my social life felt like it would be detrimental. My grand plans would have to be on hold until I could get better, and I felt frustrated and broken because of it. What I didn't know was that this injury and this time away from the life I knew would bring me so many essential reflections and lessons that I didn't even know I needed to learn. Those lessons actually ended up shaping my life to be in an even better spot professionally, personally, socially, romantically, and spiritually more than I could have ever guessed. Many of those lessons might not have been as easy for me to learn if I hadn't been in this situation.

Don't get me wrong – having to be away from the life I knew and loved, and spending so much time in isolation sucked. And yet, there were pivotal lessons I learned and re-learned that were only possible because I was isolating. This whole book is about making you think more about being happy while hermitting, but I'd have to be really ignorant to pretend that having to hermit when you don't want to doesn't suck on a very basic level. That I can't change, no matter how many great chapters I write for you. However, many of the lessons and journal prompts in this book will help you think about how you can make the best of your current situation. Even better, it will help you intentionally be better once you're out of this sucky situation.

My experience with tearing my ACL in a split-second decision at a trampoline park and in turn, spending months in isolation is the backdrop for all the lessons in this book. Every chapter will have something tied to the lessons I learned and the ways I grew through my recovery. However, I put these chapters in an order that would make sense to you, not necessarily in the order that happened in my life. Life is disorderly and chaotic, but I didn't want this book to be disorderly and chaotic for you. I prioritized your learning each lesson over chronological order. Think of it like we're both chilling on my couch and I'm telling you a whole story and lesson in itself for each chapter.

Lastly, these chapters take work. I don't expect you to plow through this book in an hour because each chapter requires you to be willing to look at parts of you that you might not have considered. Whenever you see the words "Journal Prompts," I'll have a series of questions connected to each other to get you thinking about your own situation and how it applies to what I'm teaching you. Some exercises are quick and easy. Some are a little more in depth and might need a little more time for you to think about them. Some might make you look at parts of yourself you do or don't like. However the questions feel for you, I encourage you to at least give yourself a couple minutes to really answer each question thoughtfully. No one has to see the answers but you, so I encourage you to think about the real answers even if you're ashamed of the answers. Let's practice that together now!

Introduction: Journal Prompts

What happened that's making you hermit right now? Are you doing it because you have to or are you imposing it on yourself?

How are you feeling about it? I assume you're not happy now or you wouldn't be reading a book called Happy While Hermitting, but acknowledge any feelings you have right now, even the ones that feel shitty.

How are you feeling about reading this book? You might feel ready, inspired, lame, dumb, excited, hopeful, pissed off, or any number of things. Go ahead and indulge writing about any of those feelings too.

Chapter 1:

Who Do You Think You Are? (This isn't a Threat, it's a Legitimate Question)

When I was younger and people would ask me, "What do you want to be when you grow up?" I usually didn't know how to answer the question. I was a high-performing A and B student, and each of my teachers pushed me to focus my attention on pursuing their subject. I was a coordinated athlete. I joined a private basketball team in a tournament and the parents told my dad I was "the missing link" for their team. On top of that, I was a talented soprano and sang the National Anthem at a preliminary Miss Massachusetts pageant in the seventh grade. Despite all my opportunities and displays of excellence, I had no fucking clue what I wanted to be when I grew up. All I knew was that I wanted to help people. But when grownups asked you that question, this wasn't the answer they were looking for. The expectation was that you should pick something specific. Something they could understand easily – so they would know how to judge you. The funny thing is, most people who asked me what I wanted to be when I grew up didn't actually care what my answer was, nor did they care that I changed it so many times.

Luckily, my dad was there to help me pick an answer people would want to hear. I didn't understand how biased he was towards the hard sciences until I was older. I really liked math and science, but I had a lot of other interests as well. When I mentioned to my dad that psychology was fascinating, he printed up an article explaining how most four year colleges don't prepare anyone for a job in psychology without continued education. When I got excited about the possibility of opening my own nutrition retreat center, he printed up the job instability statistics for nutritionists. When I was getting encouraged by my teachers to hone my writing skills further, he sent me an email with a link to an article on salary projections for medical editors. When I started getting interested in biomedical engineering, he sent me graphs of projected growth in that field over the next ten years. Finally, my junior year of high school, when I told him I thought I wanted to pursue civil engineering because I wanted to help rebuild infrastructure in developing communities one day, he sent me salary projections and job stability statistics through recessions for civil engineers. He couldn't have been more right about that one…. When I graduated in 2013, I graduated with an entry level job waiting for me. I was going to be able to help people right away in the career I chose.

...

In January 2017, I connected my iPhone to my new green Toyota Corolla's bluetooth and picked an upbeat song. I pulled out of the parking lot of the Boston office at my construction engineering job. I was singing at the top of my lungs, giddy with excitement. The construction company at which I had worked for the past three and a half years in Boston had an office in Michigan, working on the Little Caesars Arena. I was anticipating a life-changing call from the Michigan office any minute now. They would tell me when I would finally be transferring to the Michigan office.

Just two years prior I had fallen in love with the city of Detroit. The city was struggling hard – their population now only a fraction of their glory days. People were leaving the city for better jobs and better opportunities elsewhere. This resulted in crippling infrastructures and abandoned neighborhoods. As a construction engineer, the infinite possibilities I saw in restoring their infrastructure lit me up with excitement. However, it was the Detroit citizens' compassion and diligence that made me want to move there. They were determined to get the funding to test over ten thousand rape kits that had gone untested for years. One of their low-income neighborhoods, Brightmoor, put together a community kitchen to help make a home for small businesses in the food industry. The bustling Eastern Market, the largest farmer's market in the country, was full of local produce and small business owners that treated nearly every customer like they were their best friend. I was drawn to the culture of rebuilding their city with compassion and neighborly love, and I wanted to be a part of that community.

The Michigan branch of the construction company where I worked had several other construction jobs around the city that would make a great impact on its development, including the Little Caesars Arena. On a recent trip to Detroit, I had interviewed in person with the Michigan office. They seemed very receptive to the idea of me taking on one of a few open positions they had. They told me to take my pick for the department I wanted to be in, which led me to believe that transferring to the Michigan office was a sure bet.

As I glided down the highway, I felt a tinge of sadness mixed in with my giddy excitement. Moving to Detroit would mean leaving my thriving sidegig as a professional cuddler behind. I had thought more than once about how much happier I was seeing cuddle clients right after work than I was going to my full time job. I saw it as a possible career more than once, and even considered pursuing it full time after a Penny Hoarder article about me went viral. However, if I was moving to Detroit, I would have to rebuild a new cuddle client base. I knew that would be a full-time job in itself. I had to choose between one or the other, and Detroit had begun to fall into my lap so neatly that I picked Detroit. I had decided that if I was happier in my full time job in Detroit, it wouldn't matter what I did with professional cuddling from there.

My car radio went silent and the bluetooth flashed the caller ID. It was the Michigan branch manager! I felt my heart flutter with excitement. I took a deep breath and hit the answer button.

"Hello, Samantha Varnerin speaking."

"Hi Samantha, it's Ian."

I felt myself loosen up as I veered onto the exit ramp. "Hi Ian! Good to hear from you." I was trying to go for casual and nonchalant, but I was grinning from ear to ear. "So what's the deal with coming out there?"

I heard Ian take a sharp breath in. There was a long pause as I navigated towards the end of the exit ramp, getting closer to the traffic light at the end of it. My grin started faltering a little, my neck silently jutting out a little in anticipation. "Well," Ian started, his voice sounding a bit heavy and awkward. The light turned red before I got to it and I began to ease on the brakes when he finished what he was saying. "The positions we interviewed you for have been filled by some recent grads we hired, so we don't have a position here for you anymore."

My smile dropped as fast as my heart did. I put my foot down on the brake, creating a slight screeching sound. "What?" *I must have misheard*, I thought. "You hired recent grads instead?"

"That's correct." He sounded heavy as if those words were final.

"For the positions I was considered for?" I asked for clarity.

"That's right."

"And they're fresh out of college?"

"Yes."

"Oh," I croaked out, confused. I paused before saying much else. I couldn't believe it. I had been with the company for over three years but people fresh out of college were going to be doing the jobs I was interviewed for? I knew they had an internship-to-career program, but a summer's worth of experience didn't match my multiple years with the company. I thought all of this, but I felt it would be rude to say that out loud. Finally, I was able to say what Ian expected of me. "I understand," I choked out meekly, even though I didn't.

"I'm sorry about the trouble and I wish you the best." He quickly replied back, obviously uncomfortable with delivering his own message and wanting to get off the phone as fast as possible.

"Thank you. You too." I nearly whispered in monotone, still struck by the news and trying not to cry.

He hung up and the happy-go-lucky music automatically started up again on the radio. I let the music play for a few seconds, then shook my head and punched the radio button off. The light turned green and I got in the right lane to turn. I blinked hard, letting the tears splatter onto my cheeks in silence as I calmly drove through the intersection. This calm facade got me through the intersection as my emotions welled up in my stomach. I finally picked up the work phone that just delivered the bad news.

"What the *fucking fuck* just happened?" I shrieked as I threw the work phone in the passenger's seat and let out my rage. "I thought I had this!" I was outraged. I felt incompetent that *entry level people* were taking the jobs that I, someone nearly four years their senior, couldn't get to save her life.

"What the hell do I do now?" I yelled at the windshield while driving.

The windshield didn't answer me, but I immediately knew what the answer was going to be. My mind went back to the viral article, the several happy cuddle clients, the hundreds of aspiring cuddlers that gave me their contact info to teach them. I shook my head, but I couldn't shake this thought. Nothing was in my way now. I could build this professional cuddling job into something bigger. I felt my insides unravel as I came to this realization. *Really?* I thought. *Is this really what I'm going to do?* But I knew I didn't want to stay in construction in Boston anymore. I wanted to do this.

I knew that I was in for interesting conversations with strangers by doing professional cuddling full time. I knew I'd have to do a lot of explaining to a lot of people. I knew that people probably wouldn't take me seriously. For some reason, I anticipated being able to excel despite those efforts. After all, I had rarely failed before that point. The times I had were really hard, but those were when I was a different person in a different field. Sure, most people made assumptions about professional cuddling, but I was an *ex-*

engineer. Surely they'd listen to me and give me a chance because that title meant I must know what I'm doing, right?

I was determined to get out into the world and try gaining professional status and recognition in the community. One of my friends who was in Business Networking International (BNI) suggested I come to one of their local meetings to see if the community was right for me. BNI was for business owners sharing referrals to give to other business owners, and I figured I could give referrals to professionals and get some back in return. The members seemed fascinated with my work and I felt like they actually cared about what I did. I liked talking to other members and tried to help them by thinking about who I could refer to them well. I was confident it was a good fit, and I felt excited about joining.

That is, I *was* confident and excited until I asked the board members what the status of my application was after a meeting in May 2019. They exchanged cautious looks with each other before signaling to one of the members. I was confused when the board member pulled me to the opposite side of the room from everyone else. I realized what might have been happening and my confidence in my application began to waver. That's when he dropped the news. I blinked, taken aback a little, and then I did my best to regain my professional composure.

"What do you mean you don't know what to do with my application?" I asked him, confused at what he told me.

The board member sighed. "I don't know if we can refer anyone to you," he said. "We don't know how to do that."

I eyed him suspiciously and furrowed my brows. "Isn't that the whole point of me coming here? To *learn* how to do that?" He couldn't deny that; they had said at the meeting minutes prior that if members didn't know how to ask people for referrals, the organization had many resources that could teach you.

He kept a poker face. "Well, for example. You've been here for a few meetings. How would I refer people to you?"

This should be easy since he's a divorce lawyer, I thought. "Well, if you had a client come in and you were seeing that they weren't taking the proceedings well, you could ask them how they're feeling and–" but then I stopped when I realized what I was saying. My cheeks felt hot. No way could he have that kind of conversation with his client. That's too awkward for everyone involved, not to mention, highly unprofessional. I felt mortified that I was even suggesting it.

He shook his head when I paused, picking up on my realization. "You see? That's what I'm saying. We don't know how to best help you and we might not be able to."

I was deflated. He was right, but I wished he wasn't. I wanted to figure out some way that the conversation could be broached, but nothing came to mind. I wanted to learn, like they said other people could. But was that only possible for people that they felt comfortable with? I suddenly noticed that he was only leaning his head forward while talking to me. His feet were firmly planted further away than someone normally would while having such a serious conversation. He was clearly uncomfortable.

I walked out of the room and saw a few other people from the BNI meeting. One of the older men saw me and then put his head on the guy next to him and wrapped his arms around the poor unsuspecting fellow. They both looked at me with smiles as the older man made an exaggerated sigh, appearing to enjoy cuddling his buddy's shoulder. The group of men chuckled as I approached.

I felt sick when I realized they were mocking me. *They don't take me seriously,* I realized. I wasn't networking with them at all this whole time. Reflecting back on the previous meetings I attended, I now felt like I was the weird kid that showed up to their grownups' small business meeting. I fascinated them, which is why they were interested in what I had to say, but hardly any of them thought I was really a business owner. These two men pretending to cuddle in front of me made that very clear.

For the next year and a half, I hustled to make my business shine. If networking meant people wouldn't take me seriously or listen to me, I'd do everything else. I slowly climbed forward, slowly building a consistent client base up from putting out Google ads, blogging about my work, getting local and national publicity, and listing myself on a bunch of other cuddle websites. Suddenly I was getting clients coming in that told me their friend had met me at a networking event and told me how silly my work sounded. While they nodded along with their friend laughing about how ridiculous of a business I had, my clients were quietly and discreetly Googling my business name to find me. Despite agreeing with their friend in public, they felt distant from their friends and others around them. Hiring someone to cuddle with them sounded like a great way to not feel as lonely anymore. The people that would never hire me were suddenly becoming my best word-of-mouth advertisers.

By the end of 2018, I felt like I was really making progress and that people were seeing me for who I really was. I was becoming even more independent! I had made plans in December to have a great year ahead of me to grow my business and keep on working hard. I was ready to sprint in 2019 for teaching other cuddlers more, working with more clients, building a really great practice, and being more of who I was! That is, I was ready to sprint until I couldn't walk anymore when I officially injured myself in January.

My sudden inability to work, walk and be independent crippled me more than physically. I lost all sense of my independence from that injury. For the first week in bed, I ruminated over how I could have stopped myself from getting injured, how this would affect me for months, how I would keep any of my clients, what the hell I would do for money with a gimp knee the size of a football, and many other bejumbled thoughts. I felt mentally and physically exhausted going over everything, and I took frequent naps as I tortured myself with these questions. But the one thought that popped up more often than the other ones was this question of what this helplessness meant about me. *Who am I if I can't take care of myself?* When I finally called my mom to ask her to take me in while I tried to support myself, I felt like I had lost all sense of independence. What kind of independent person does that?

When my mom brought me to her house after that first week, I spent a few days really questioning who I was if I couldn't do the things I was doing before. Sure, this was temporary, but what if it changed who I am forever? I liked who I was before my injury. What if I could never get back to that point? What if having to rely on everyone meant that I was a burden to everyone around me? More importantly, what did being too injured and helpless to even make myself a meal mean about who I am? I lived with my Inner Critic yelling at me, unsure what to make of our identity in this out-of-our-control situation.

• • •

"I'm terrible," I muttered for the umpteenth time from my mother's first floor master bedroom at 1pm the third day I was there.

"No you're not. You're injured." My mom repeated for the umpteenth time back, irate as she shook the creases out of a thin, grey blanket. She held it on one end as the blanket floated over me and slowly fell over my body. She smoothed it out before I went down for a nap. "Can you stop telling yourself that?"

I sighed and rolled my eyes. "Okay," I groaned, 100% not ready to stop telling myself that. I was tired and spiraling, but if the past three days at my parents' house was an indicator, I knew I'd feel a little more like myself once I took a nap. My eyes got heavy and I felt tired, but I didn't feel any better yet. My mind was still battling itself, trying to figure out who we were and what kind of person we were supposed to be since we couldn't do any of the things we normally would do. I turned to my phone, Googling "How to be yourself when you can't walk." I desperately scrolled through unrelated articles for an answer and found none. I began nodding off in front of my phone until I finally put it away and I slowly slipped into unconsciousness.

···

The next morning, I woke up and felt my calves ache. I remembered what the doctor had said about knee injuries: oftentimes the calf tends to compensate to keep stability in the leg. It felt so sore and pained, and I felt the inclination to stretch it. The tightness reminded me of the beginning of my high school track seasons – I'd constantly get calf spasms from how weak they got from no conditioning training. *I guess I'm weak now, too,* I sighed as I pointed and flexed my toes, trying to get blood flowing to my calves to make them feel better. I massaged the sides of my knee, still the size of a softball from the swelling. I needed to get some ice and breakfast soon.

A few minutes later, I hobbled out of the bedroom on my crutches, the hardwood floor faintly creaking as I slowly made my way out. I saw my mom playing Candy Crush from her phone around the half wall as I made my way. She looked up as she heard me, but I saw her eyes dart down to the ground too. I knew that must have meant that she didn't so much hear me as much see what her adorable but skittish black cat, Romeo, did on the other side of the half wall when he heard me.

I was convinced that Romeo had short term memory loss and trusted nothing he didn't see every day. He had acted scared around me ever since my mom adopted him while I was in college. No matter how many times I came home to visit and no matter how many times I tried to say hi to him, he was always ready to spring away from me. I was clearly not the Juliet to his Romeo in the slightest. Because he never remembered me and clearly didn't like me, I wasn't surprised when I turned the corner from the half wall and saw him staring right back at me in a familiar weird frog pose. He was almost ready to spring out of sight upon seeing me with my crutches in hand. How dare I bring these foreign objects anywhere near him, after all! He sat back and put his front paws on the arm of my mom's red loveseat, about to make a run for it as I got closer to the lazy chair next to him.

Romeo's eyes' followed me intently as I made my way to the seat designated for my leg's support. He kept looking down at my crutches and up to where my hand met the foam cushion to hold them. He did not trust me at all, and those crutches looked scary. No one had purposely hit him in the seven years that he lived with this family, but he seemed to think that today was going to be the day that these crutches would try to murder him in cold blood. As I began turning my butt towards the seat to sit down, I turned back to see if he was still on the loveseat arm next to my chair. I made one reach for the crutches to rest them against the loveseat, the only place I could comfortably stand them up and reach them while sitting. Just as I did, Romeo sprung off the armchair onto the floor, scurrying around the corner to my mom's room and out of sight.

I raised my eyebrows at my mom as she chuckled. I didn't notice she had stopped playing her game to watch this short spectacle. "He's still scared of you," she said, trying to stifle her amusement at Romeo's skittishness around me.

I rolled my eyes, unimpressed. "He doesn't like me. He hasn't since you got him." I was used to this routine with Romeo since my senior year of college when my mom adopted him: I would come into a room, he would look at me scared, and he'd run away as soon as I got too close. "He's a dick."

"No," she defended, "he's just a scaredy cat."

"Yeah, that's true," I said. "But this happens with a lot of cats for me. He's just a really extreme example." I stretched my neck out in the lazy chair, trying to see if he was creeping back out again around the half wall. "I do want him to like me, but maybe I'm too much of a dog personality for him," I pondered. I've called myself a "dog personality" for years because, unlike Romeo, dogs on leashes would pull towards me to say hi to me even if I wasn't paying attention to them. I seemed to attract dogs and repel cats more often than not.

A few minutes after settling into my chair, I saw Romeo slowly creep back out, meowing short, high-pitched noises at my mom. "Come on up," my mom cooed, patting the spot on her lap. He cautiously sauntered across the floor, eyeing me to make sure I didn't move. I held my breath while he did so because I was afraid of prompting him to make a run for it again. As he finally reached my mom, he gracefully hopped up on the couch and began walking across her lap, lowering himself to get a pet on his head and his back again and again.

My mom gave him a hug as he stood on her lap and she nuzzled him. "I love you, kitty," she continued cooing. He meowed a barely audible meow and started nuzzling his own head into my mom's face.

I laughed. "I guess it doesn't matter what I do, does it?" I said. "He can sense who I am, and I'm a scary, super friendly girl!" I put my hands up and jerked forward towards Romeo, and as I did he snapped his head to me and bristled in my mom's arms, his claws visible. My mom winced a little for him and I laughed so hard I snort laughed. "Dogs love me, and he hates the shit out of me. I don't care at all though."

When I said "I don't care at all though," something clicked in my head. Romeo was judging me like others did, but I didn't actually care what Romeo thought of me. To Romeo, what I did and what I was capable of didn't matter to him either. Whatever role I claimed to have or how independent I was didn't make him like me more. Being helpless right now didn't impact how he felt about me either (although he clearly hated the crutches). He most likely thought I was the "Scary Girl with Metal Thing That Is Definitely Going to Murder Me" regardless of how I showed up to him. That interpretation, however, was not true and I knew that. I felt confident that I wasn't that and felt good about it.

Why was how I felt about myself not invoking strong emotions in me? I felt angry and defiant when I got passed up for the transfer to Detroit. When I got rejected from BNI and mocked, I felt embarrassed and unprofessional. I began to feel on top of the world when I was seeing higher and higher success for my professional cuddling practice. But when I got injured and couldn't do anything for myself, I felt defeated and useless. All of these were strong emotions, and yet when Romeo showed extreme anxiety being around me I was only mildly sad about it. All of these are valid feelings, but what about how I was looking at these things made me feel so strongly about some things but not others? I continued looking at Romeo occasionally eyeing me while he attempted to relax in my mom's lap, pushing his butt towards her face sometimes. My mom then said something so random and disturbing that somehow tied all my thoughts together.

"You horny boy," my mom cooed and laughed at Romeo, pushing his butt upwards towards her face.

"Mom, *what*?" I jerked my head up from my inner ramblings.

"He's horny," she repeated, pointing to his butt in her face.

"Mom," I started, my eyes a bit disturbed at my mom's conclusion. "Romeo came fixed, didn't he? That's not possible. I think cats do that because that's their way of showing that they trust you."

"Really?" She said, seemingly shocked at this new information that her cat isn't overtly thirsty towards her.

"Yeah," I said, still horrified at my mom's misguided conclusion. "My friends and I Googled this a while ago. This is a common occurrence for house cats that trust their owners."

"Oh," she replied, taking in this new knowledge with Romeo still showing her his butt. We had an awkward silence between us, me not sure what to make of this incredibly awkward exchange with my mom. She eventually scratched just above his tail. "You're weird," she said to him. Romeo, not understanding any of this strange conversation that just happened, continued raising his butt and showing his behind to my mom. He still trusted my mom because that's who he is.

...

Unlike Romeo who doesn't understand (and probably doesn't care) when someone judges him, we mostly aren't immune to what other people think of us. Despite knowing other people's opinions aren't always true, we tend to take in what we hear as truth, whether we personally believe that about ourselves or not. These projected beliefs tend to shape how we show up, whether we're trying to fight against those judgements or whether we're accepting that we can't change them. When I got injured, I couldn't change that I was injured. However, I interpreted that I was useless because I couldn't work or support myself. It wasn't until I saw Romeo treat me like shit that I realized these thoughts were simply an interpretation of my situation, not a reflection of my character. When my mom completely misinterpreted Romeo's butt peepshow as an XXX-rated moment instead of the innocent sign of trust that it was, I realized how easily some of these interpretations can completely miss the mark compared to the reality.

I had to strip away all of the superficial ideas I had about myself. If I wasn't a professional cuddler, an engineer, an independent woman, or even a person that could walk without her knee and calf killing her, who was I? The reality was simple: those things didn't matter. I had to say "fuck that" to all of those thoughts and really get to what it is that's important to me.

If you're feeling like you don't matter because you're not able to go to the places you want to or do the things you want to, that doesn't mean anything about who you are as a person. In fact, a focus on who you really are starts not in what you do or what other people think of you. I focused on what other people thought of me for far too long and kept finding myself sidetracked by other people's expectations, I even imposed many expectations on myself. Instead, taking the situation at face value – this happened, you're stuck, and this sucks – is the only piece that's factual. Who you are as a result of this is not necessarily true.

Who you really think you are is ultimately based around what's important to you. It requires digging deeper into what your values are. When you can get clear on what's really important to you at the essence of your being, you can show up in any situation more stable and more clear on what you can do next. To figure out what those things are, say "fuck that" to whatever superficial things you think are important – what you do for a living, what your peers think of you, your mad sports skills, where you live, how much money you make, how dependent or independent you're supposed to be – because all of those can change at any time. What's important to you can change too, but those things are more at the core of your being. And let's worry instead about what's at the core of your being. What's behind all the fancy titles, accolades, investment accounts, and expectations you or others have for yourself? Who are you? What are you? The more you can get a handle of what kind of person you are without any ego-stroking status symbols to cling onto, the more fluid and adaptable you'll be in any situation.

In the end, what I realized was the essence of my being boiled down to some less specific things about myself, and it had to do with how I wanted to show up in every situation: I was determined. I was resourceful. I was energetic. I was inquisitive. I was caring. The more I thought about these words to describe myself, the more I realized that these carry over into everything I do in my life. It didn't matter what role I took on because I still carried who I was everywhere. These ways of looking at myself were the essence of who I was.

Chapter 1: Journal Prompts

What are some things that you've used to mean something about you? Include titles, other people's opinions, where you live, salaries, relationships, things you own, sports or activities you do, etc.

Cross out anything you've listed above that got taken away from you (or severely limited compared to normal times) through this need to isolate. For example, if you had to stop working while isolated, circle your job. Then write in the blank below how you feel not having those things.

Now write out this sentence in the blank space below with every circled item you have. Make more spaces if you need to

I don't need _____ to be me.

I don't need _____ to be me.

I don't need _____ to be me.

I don't need _____ to be me.

Now that those are out of the way, let's get to who you really are. Circle the words that you feel describe you and/or write in some of your own:

Kind   lifelong learner   Generous   Friendly
        Resourceful   Creative   Artistic

Determined   Loud   Introspective   Understanding
        Problem-solver   Adventurous

Intuitive   Intentional   Nurturing   Strong-willed
        Innovative   Performer

How can you, in the situation you're in right now, still be any of the things you circled above? If you're stuck, try this sentence stem: I can be more _____ by doing more _____.

Chapter 2:

Letting Your Body Hit The Floor is so 2001

I have a confession: I was – and still am – a chronic workaholic. I have been for as far back as I can remember. I pursue between two to five major projects at time with as much intensity as I can muster. This multi-passionate way of living and my high-achiever tendencies meant I was easily sold on #hustle culture. #hustle meant that I could spend my twenty somethings and my seemingly limitless energy on working as hard as I could so I could reap the benefits later. I got entranced with the idea of setting aside everything else in my life to focus on building a dream business, paying down debt, and achieving financial freedom so as to not have to work as hard later in life. I wanted to fulfill so many dreams, and I didn't want to have to choose what to pursue. Instead of making hard choices on what to pursue, I would pursue everything all at once and work as hard as humanly possible to get all the things I want.

Unfortunately, when we decide to go for ALL of the things we want at once, something has usually got to give. For me, that something ended up being my basic human needs. I would habitually underestimate how much time and energy I needed to set aside in order to pursue my dreams (and I still do). And I'd often overestimate how much I could do. To make more time, I'd constantly burn out by hyperfocusing on the task at hand to the point where I would do nothing else while working on it. I'd later come out of a work stupor having missed several meals and being terribly sleep-deprived. Friends would try to encourage me to step away, but I usually just saw their concern as them not understanding me or what I was sacrificing for. I mean, I was trying to get promoted! I was running two side businesses. I was trying to move to Detroit. Unfortunately, my friends were right; *I* was the one who didn't understand what I was really sacrificing. The extent of my burnout became clear in late 2015 when I couldn't tell if I was falling asleep or fainting at night.

In October 2015, I came-to in a cold sweat on my living room floor. My head jerked up after leaning against the arm of the couch for hours of unconscious, restless sleep. My heart thudded loudly in my chest as I sat up straight... *Am I late?* I thought. I wasn't sure if I was, but it was my immediate first thought. I looked outside and it was pitch black. *What time is it?* I wondered. I checked my phone. 11:32pm. Middle of the night. I let out a breath I didn't know I was holding in. I felt my heartbeat slow down. Somehow it was calming and not unsettling that I woke up on the floor and not in my bed. My mind quickly switched gears and focused on what I had in front of me. *I still have six and a half more hours before I need to get ready for work in the morning,* I thought. I wiped my brow of the cold, sticky liquid that was collecting on my temples. I took a deep breath in and let it out slowly, trying to focus on what I was working on before I passed out. Or did I fall asleep? Either way, I felt my head begin to sway and throb trying to think more about it. My stomach grumbled angrily from deep emptiness and I felt weak. Hunger pangs. *When was the last time I ate?* I tried to remember. I had a quick dinner the day before last, but that couldn't have been the last time I ate, was it?

My stomach continued protesting. *Do I have any food in the house?* I stood up slowly, my equilibrium still off. I searched my cabinets for something quick, realizing that the sooner I could stop feeling like this the more productive I could be. I found a granola bar. I ripped open the foil wrapping and inhaled it, trying to piece my thoughts together so I could start working. My stomach grumbled some more, yearning for more food. *I need to eat more before I can do anything else. Is the pizza place next to the college still open?* I tapped my phone screen to find their website. It said it was open until 1am. I sighed, trying to temper my demanding stomach while I poured myself a glass of water. I gulped it down, bundled up in my jacket and scarf, and strode out the door to the pizza place to satiate my stomach. I would get a calorie-laden calzone that my body would all but absorb immediately.

That was the fifth night in two weeks that I wasn't sure if I had fainted or fallen asleep on the couch. It happened every couple of nights during that two week timeframe in October. It became almost routine: I would wake up from the couch or the floor of my living room at some point after 11pm, unsure what to do because I couldn't bring myself to work anymore but I didn't have food in the house to feed my literal starvation. Reflecting on this particular time period, I'm disturbed at how automatically I'd get up, try to find food in my house, go to the pizza place down the street and eat at odd hours of the night. Even as it was happening I knew it was not normal or healthy that this kept happening, but at some point I had accepted that this was my life now. I had adapted so quickly to letting my body just hit the floor, it felt eerie how effortless it was to exchange a healthy personal life for the dreams I had for myself.

...

      It turns out that any semblance of a good lifestyle wasn't all I gave up. Ironically, I also gave up being productive. After this two week period of living like a zombie, I blamed my lack of focus like it was an inherent virtue I lacked. My therapist had suggested that I might have ADHD based on what I was telling her. Though I always joked that I might have ADHD growing up, hearing her say that felt oddly freeing and validating that maybe the problem wasn't me being lazy and tired until I finally woke my ass up at 11pm on weekdays. So I went in to get testing for ADHD from a psychologist. I thought that getting this testing and diagnosis was going to help me figure out how I could focus better. I didn't know that I could be having the issues I was having because I was *too* good at focusing.

      In December 2015, I was in my psychologist's office in Roxbury. She had administered my ADHD examination. To no one's surprise, I had ADHD. That part of the reveal felt like a formality, but I really just wanted to know how I could be more productive again. I listened to her suggestions to improve my symptoms actively. She mentioned that people with ADHD tend to do something called hyperfocusing, which was a fancy way of saying that they work on something and focus so much that they forget about everything else in their life. It was when she mentioned this that she casually said the biggest wake-up call I had in my adult life.

      "Some might find themselves in a hospital bed due to forgetting essential things in their life." She waved her hand nonchalantly as if she were commenting on the weather.

      I perked up. *That* sounded important to know. "I'm sorry, what?" I asked.

      "It's quite common for adults with ADHD that hyperfocus too much to forget to eat or sleep properly," she continued. "If left unchecked, it could escalate to needing medical attention."

      My eyes went wide. *If I don't do something, I could be passing out and wake up in a hospital bed instead of on my couch.* That was the wakeup call I needed to turn my self-care around. I needed to stop worrying about hustling all the time and instead worry about me.

...

For years after I received my ADHD diagnosis, I was determined to find the balance between making my dreams come true and taking care of my body. One of my psychologist's suggestions was to have at least one quick meal in the house when I didn't have time to make food. I slowly got better about eating regularly, and shortly after, I dated someone who helped me get back on track with eating, sleeping and exercising properly. But within six months I found myself getting pulled back to my old habits of overestimating what I could do and underestimating how long it would take me to do it. I wasn't passing out on my living room floor anymore, but I was ramping back up again and wearing myself down fast. I seemed to be repeating this cycle every three to six months.

At the beginning of 2019, I confessed to my life coach of two years that this was an ongoing problem I kept running into. She might as well have said "No shit, Sam" because this didn't come as a surprise to her at all. Instead, she's a decent human being and she said something else.

"Sam, there is no rush."

"I know that," I said.

"By rushing yourself everywhere and trying to do everything all the time, you're not actually enjoying this work, are you?"

I thought about it. She was right. I really didn't enjoy even pushing myself into the ground usually, but here I was falling into the habit of pushing myself again and again. As I pushed myself once more, I found myself enjoying it less and less. At what point did I start associating work with overloading myself with everything and rushing to get it all done?

She encouraged me to try to ground myself more and slow down. In early January, I decided to pick a word that would be my guiding principle for the rest of the year. "Grounded" felt like the right word to me, and my coach loved it. We both felt it was a word that would help me slow down more and be more intentional with how I move in the world. I wrote it on a whiteboard in my bedroom and wrote it in my notebook.

Of course, less than a week later was when I tore my ACL and I was "grounded" in a way I didn't plan to be. I was pretty bitter about the word almost mocking me on my whiteboard for the week I was stuck helpless in my room, unable to walk unsupported. I started giving my whiteboard the middle finger when I saw the word, but I didn't erase it. Every time I opened up my notebook to write more of my scattered thoughts down, I saw the word "grounded" as well and started to hate it. My mind got restless and I felt useless not working when I got transferred over to my parents' house to recover.

After sustaining such a severe injury, I knew I needed to let myself rest so I could work with clients again – so that's what I did. The problem was, I still didn't know how to let myself rest *enough*. Just two days before my surgery, I made this master plan to go through five different online courses I had bought years ago. My plan included watching the videos from each program and taking color-coded notes. I figured if I was just waiting to be able to walk, taking a few modules of online courses a day should be easy. I smiled and approved my own lesson plans to start the day after my surgery. I put the notebook with my lesson plans away next to my nightstand, ready to pick it up after I returned from the hospital.

I had no idea how unrealistically ambitious that plan was until I tried doing it. It would have been an amazing master plan under normal circumstances. But in this case, I was about to deal with a month and a half of being away from everyone I loved except my parents. I was going to be on mind-altering, highly addictive painkillers that were going to inhibit my ability to mentally function properly. And most importantly, I was about to go through the intensive experience of physically recovering from *getting my old ACL taken out and putting a new ACL from a dead person in its place.* Not one of these factors alone could be considered "normal" circumstances, nevermind dealing with all three at once. If I could go back in time and talk to myself at this point, I would shake myself and tell myself to stop focusing on anything other than healing after a *major fucking surgery.*

...

The day after my surgery, I woke up in my parents home feeling sore and tired, yet motivated to do something productive while I was immobile. I was convinced I would be able to immediately get started on a course about using a project management software for solopreneurs. *If nothing else*, I thought, *this will help me organize everything else in my life.* I opened my laptop and sat up, my knee still wrapped up in an ice pack attached to an ice machine to ease the swelling constantly. Somehow, I was able to focus and take notes on this course for two hours.

Although those first hours were smooth sailing, it started going downhill quickly afterward. The pain in my knee became unbearable and I needed another painkiller. I took one with lunch and turned back to my screen, my sandwich still in hand, to watch some more video modules. I was just getting into color coding my notes when suddenly, my eyes felt heavy and I felt this warmth spread across my head. My mind began floating away from the speaker's voice I was listening to and onto… nothing. I wasn't focused on anything. My mind felt big but empty, but oddly happy. I was also feeling really tired. I shut the laptop and pushed it aside to make room in my bed for me to lay down and close my eyes. Within a few minutes, I was unconscious.

When I woke up, it was about three hours later. *Wow, that was a long nap*, I thought. *I thought I had slept pretty well last night.* I reached for my laptop on the other side of the king size bed, but then I felt my head. My mind felt foggy and unfocused. *I don't think I can bring myself to do more of this right now*, I thought. *I want to, but I can't.* So instead, I picked up my phone and played a game.

For the next month or so, I didn't do much work other than sending a few emails with some updates here and there. Whenever my mind had ideas for projects to take on in my business and I tried to do more writing or digital product creation, my body would pull me back into resting. My desire to push and hustle was in direct conflict with my body's desire to simply heal. It felt like my body was telling me "Bitch, give me a break. Seriously, haven't I earned that in the 28 years of dealing with your crap yet?" I was surprisingly accepting of my body's demands, and I quickly found myself trying to look out for it first. My main focus had to be on my body.

After I got off the painkillers, my priority became sleeping better so my body could heal. I got some energy healing and my mom brought me balanced meals to load me up on nutrients. Having meals regularly and sleeping at regular intervals was foreign to me since I tended to simply work until I couldn't anymore. I started to get used to going to bed at normal times and eating at certain times of the day, two things my body probably wanted from me all along but I couldn't hear it screaming at me until it was too late.

One evening about a week after surgery, I was looking over my documents of what activities I should be able to do soon. It said I was another 1-2 weeks away from being able to walk anywhere without crutches. That felt incredibly far away, but at that point, the message from my life coach was starting to sink in: *there is no rush.* At that point I was complacent and accepting that my body needed to move at its own pace and I needed to do what I could to support it in the meantime. I wasn't happy nor sad about it, but I was more just soldiering on with the understanding that taking care of me should be what I hyperfocus on. I read the documents, still holding them in my hands, and I walked to the bathroom.

Once I lowered myself onto the toilet, I realized something vital was missing, but I couldn't figure out what it was. Did I put my brace back on before I got up? Yeah, that was on correctly. Were my Ace bandages on my leg? Yes, those were wrapped securely around them too. Sneakers? I had my laceless sneakers on so that wasn't an issue. What the hell did I not bring to the bathroom? It wasn't until I finished up and tried to get myself up that I realized what I forgot: *my crutches.*

Holy shit! I thought. *I just walked the fifteen steps from the bed to the bathroom without using my crutches or holding onto walls! And I didn't even think about it! And my body isn't screaming at me!* With this miraculous feeling of triumph building in my chest, I finally started yelling battle victory cries. My parents began rushing to the bathroom in a panic, worried I've seriously hurt myself.

"What's wrong?!" My mom shrilled, her eyes wild and my dad hanging back, both scared of what they would both find but immediately relieved to see I wasn't writhing in pain.

"I did it," I panted out, tears beginning to form in my eyes while standing up. "What did I forget to bring to the bathroom?"

My mom looked around. My dad furrowed his eyebrows, standing in the short foyer between the master bedroom and master bathroom. Then their eyes landed on my crutches. Their eyes went wide.

"How did you– ?"

"I don't know. I just forgot them," I smiled wide. "But it was like nothing. I shouldn't even be walking like this for another week."

"Well, don't overdo it yet," my dad cautioned, bringing me my crutches. "You've been allowed to bear weight on it with the crutches, but still use them for now."

I rolled my eyes. I fully intended to keep using the crutches until my medical team told me I could stop. I knew better than to go against what the doctors told me to do. But this moment was key to me seeing the results of what happened when I let my body rest the way it wanted to instead of pushing it harder and ignoring what it needs. This moment reminded me that by giving my body the basic care it needed, it was able to heal and strengthen and grow.

...

While my ACL recovery seemed fast to most people, my physical therapist told me I was right on schedule and that everyone else just sucked at doing what the doctors tell them to do (thank you for forcing me to listen to the doctors, body!). I continued to strengthen my knee slowly in physical therapy twice a week. I could feel my muscles come back and get stronger, and I felt less helpless. I didn't need to use the crutches for walking around anymore. Eventually, my physical therapist gave me permission to take off my brace when I was simply doing tasks indoors. This big leap was the stamp of approval I needed to start working with cuddle clients again! I was so excited to finally be able to work again.

There was no way in hell my parents would let me have clients (read: stranger dangers) in their home, and I wasn't confident that I could go see clients in their homes while I was still recovering. This meant I was going to have to see clients in my apartment in Boston like I did before I got injured. However, I grew attached to my physical therapist near my parents' house after seeing them twice a week for two months. Trying to find a new physical therapist to help me finish my recovery now seemed like a bad idea, but I still needed to see my physical therapist twice a week. At this point, I couldn't choose between not working (especially since I was flat broke from not working for two and a half months) or not focusing on my body. In the end, I found a middle ground that would let me have both.

...

"Hi mom!" I called out as I opened my parents' front door at 7pm on the first Tuesday in May. I was still a little weak in the knees from my intensive water aerobics at physical therapy moments before. I could smell the scent of my mom's salmon recipe from the door and I got excited. I plopped my leg with my brace on through the doorway first before following with my good leg. As I did so, I saw a little black ball speed across the floor away from me. I chuckled at Romeo's skittishness.

"Hi Sammy!" my mom called back. "Ready for dinner?"

This was how we went about our weeks for the past month: I would go down to the Cape for my physical therapy appointments on Tuesday evenings and stay with my parents until Thursday morning when I had my second physical therapy appointment. After that second appointment on Thursdays, I would drive back up to Boston and work with clients in my home until the following Tuesday. Essentially, this meant that for three days of the week I focused more on my body than my work, and the other four days of the week I'd focus on my work a little more than my body. Somehow, this forced focal point I had when going down to my parents' house and seeing my physical therapist created this sense of balance for my entire week.

Interestingly enough, I found myself still working at my parents' house when I went back, but not right away. Instead, I'd go to their place and take care of myself first. I'd shower, have dinner, and talk with my mom and dad. I'd go for a walk around the neighborhood or attempt to take pictures of Romeo before he could run away from me again. I'd have a snack, do some journaling, and breathe slower and deeper. At some point on Wednesday late morning or afternoon, I'd perk up and get ready to do an hour or two of focused, productive work. I worked fewer hours than I ever had in my business before that month. Somehow, despite my lighter workload, I made the same amount of money as I had before my injury when I was tired and hustling all the time. The only difference was that I felt better.

...

Look, I love early 2000's hard rock as much as any secret emo kid stuck in an adult body, but when "Let the Bodies Hit The Floor" becomes your theme song for the #hustle life like it was for me – you might need to make more space to take care of yourself. Even if you're not self-sacrificial to that extreme, being in isolation can easily breed an opportunity to either loosen taking care of ourselves or to give more space to it. If you're bored enough or ambitious enough, it's usually the former over the latter. You might even feel inspired to take on a new project or one you've put off, and I encourage you to do that! At first, you might be lit up about this chance to do new things, but after about a week or two you might find yourself slipping back into old habits like I did. If your default isn't to take care of yourself, you're in trouble.

Really, your body is a lot like a baby. It'll cry about any kind of discomfort it has, but it doesn't speak the same language we do. If we don't give it the rest and space it needs, you might really see your body hit the floor and end up in a hospital. If you're anything like me, you didn't sign up to be attached to a baby 24/7 and you're mad that you have to treat your body like one. But I promise you it's easier to hear what your baby of a body is asking for from you when you're not trying to fill all your time with shit to do that no one's asking you to do.

You can fill some of your time with projects and fun things to do, but leave some time for resting and taking care of you. And by some time, I mean way more than you're probably comfortable with. If you're isolated and can't see anyone, it sucks, and trying to keep yourself busy for too many hours will start to serve more like a distraction from any healing you need to do (physical or emotional). So make sure you prioritize that more than anything else with a shit ton more hours than you spend doing work you didn't have to sign up for.

Chapter 2: Journal Prompts

What do you want to do when you're resting or taking care of your body during this time by yourself? List whatever comes to mind. Meditation, napping, showering, putting on lotion, cooking, etc.

When will you do it? Will it be the same time every day or different times? If different, list them out for Monday, Tuesday, Wednesday, etc.

Now try doubling the amount of time you spend resting and taking care of yourself. How would you fit that into your schedule if you had to? More often than not, this is the real amount of rest we probably need.

Life happens and we need to take care of important things, but our time to rest gets shafted when we do that. How will you know when you need to let yourself rest more?

Chapter 3: Make Your Inner Critic Work With You, Not Against You

Growing up, I spent a lot of time relying on other people to validate how I felt about myself. The way I performed in school was a big piece of my childhood self-worth. I took the things others thought of me as absolute truth, rather than looking within to find confidence or self-worth. Since doing something good earned me a lot of praise, I was constantly striving to be better. The better I did, the more praise and validation I got from my parents, friends, and childhood sweethearts. But when I didn't do well, the praise or encouragement seemed to dissipate into long, uncomfortable silences.

Bad soccer game? – I had an uncomfortably silent ride in the car alone with my dad.

Brought home a bad test grade? – My mom tossed the paper to the corner passive aggressively without a word, and went back to whatever she was doing.

Friends got mad at me for not agreeing with them? – I got the cold shoulder from them at lunch, and would have to spend half the period in the bathroom.

Talked too much to that guy in French class – the one my boyfriend was jealous of? – I got completely ignored until he was ready to tell me what I did wrong, (usually several classes later if that day at all).

When this happened over and over again, I started wondering what was wrong with me.

Today I recognize that this was how most of the people around me coped with their intense emotions instead of expressing their anger out loud and hurting me. After all, my mom taught me "If you don't have anything nice to say, don't say anything at all." But the problem with that way of living is that if someone said nothing, I *knew* they wanted to say something bad about me. Without the silent culprit there to speak up, my Inner Critic began to speak for them. And let me tell you, she was a real bitch. Even if I was confident and caring towards myself and others, my Inner Critic was really good at reminding me that what I was doing was a front because I was secretly selfish, lazy, and a terrible human being.

My Inner Critic continued like this, unfiltered, for years – hacking away at my self-esteem and sense of value, despite the many good things I was trying to do in the world. She convinced me that I was a burden to people because I was not sacrificing myself constantly or being the best person I possibly could be at any given time. I would work myself to the bone, exhausting myself to my wit's end. I hated her and how she made me feel. It wasn't until I was twenty-five when I started questioning her. Once I did, I realized she didn't have good enough answers for me. She was really good at fighting me, but what I really needed was for her to fight *for* me.

•••

I turned my car engine off and took a deep sigh in my parking spot at the gym. It was my fourth time there this week. My job site let me get out early in February 2016, which meant I could get to the gym before most people got out of work. *Good thing, too*, my Inner Critic said. *Don't want the fit people to see your ugly ass.* I cut the engine with one hand and swooped up my green gym bag with the other. I hugged the bag towards my chest, hiding my round belly. I couldn't help but notice my sides protruded from behind it still. *You're still fucking fat, bitch. Look at this.*

One reason I even got this gym membership was because the number I saw on the scale was higher than I had ever seen before. Of course, my Inner Critic always had a lot to say about whenever I gained weight... and none of it was kind. But this time I gained weight in 2016 was different. This time I had a new boyfriend unlike anyone I had ever dated at that point before and he had something to say about it too. Every year before this one, whomever I dated didn't say anything about my weight even if I said something about it. I did not expect him to say what he did without mincing it at all.

"I can't bring you home to my mom if you're that fat."

Those words echoed in my head and haunted me. My Inner Critic raged with a strange melancholy victory, and I felt sick to my stomach. *Of course he can't,* my Inner Critic went off. *He used to be a personal trainer. He's used to being around people caring about their bodies. You kind of do, but clearly not enough.*

Okay, I replied. Now I have a goal to work towards.

Yes you do. Just look at you. He's probably used to associating with titans. You're no titan. More of a Telletubby.

I became aware of my hips protruding from behind my bag. I guess you're right, I sighed, walking down the stairs to the underground gym. I opened the door to loud, upbeat music. I tapped my membership card on the monitor, my Inner Critic grumbling incoherent insecurities as I walk towards the locker room, noticing other people's eyes catch me along the way. *They must be judging me*, I thought. I slouch a bit and beeline to the locker room where the hard working gym rats and gym bunnies can't see me. Everyone was so fit, so skinny, so muscular. I was none of those things.

I eyed my typical locker in the corner, pushed away from everyone else. Another young woman was changing about a foot next to it. She stretched her arms straight up over her head, her bright pink crop top showing her flat, ripped stomach and a gentle hourglass curve. Between her exposed stomach and her skin tight yoga pants, I winced at the full awareness that my body looked nothing like that, but I really wanted it to. I need to find another locker today, I thought. Being next to her will feel like torture.

I picked a locker further away from the entrance, but not without catching the woman's attention. She widened her eyes, then chuckled. Is she laughing at me? I thought. Is it that ridiculous that I'm in the gym trying to make myself look anything like you?

Yeah, that is ridiculous, my inner critic grumbled. *She's thinking 'Good luck, bitch. Why are we even here? Just because you bought a gym membership doesn't mean you belong here.'*

I slid open my phone. My new boyfriend sent me a text with a link to today's workout for me. Bicep and chest supersets and ab workouts. As I bent down to tie my sneakers, I felt the soreness in my quads from yesterday's leg day workout. I covered my ears with my big bulky over-ear headphones, pressing the volume button up to nearly full volume. *That won't distract you from your gross body,* my Inner Critic clicked her metaphorical tongue at me as I tried to fight through it.

Before I left the locker room to go to my grueling beatdown of a workout, I took one quick look in the mirror. I felt my chest tighten and my stomach churn a little as I saw my own "gross body." Puffy cheeks from fat, flabby arms that squeezed awkwardly into the sleeves, a stomach with several rolls bigger than my chest when I put on my shorts, and weird indents around where my bra lines are showing just how much bigger than my bra I really am. These were things I had noticed before, thanks to my Inner Critic, but thanks to the fresh words from my new boyfriend, she's even more adamant about making sure I'm paying attention to this. She did a good job imitating his voice while making pig jokes in my head about each body part I paid attention to.

I winced, then I took a swig of my water and gripped the bottle. *I'll show you*, I thought. *I'm not going to be fat anymore. I'm going to be like that skinny girl. I'm going to get there and everyone is going to be shocked. And then I'll be happy.*

...

In June 2016, I thought I achieved that happiness. I had put in so much work between doing the bodybuilding workouts and eating better. I was performing better at work. I lost fifteen pounds and it was noticeable. My boyfriend and I had bought new clothes together that he helped me pick out. We were planning on driving out to Park Slope that weekend and we'd meet his mother and the rest of his family. He was even coming onto me every time he saw me and our sex was on *fire*. I was working on being able to do pull ups, something I've never been able to do in my life. I felt like my life was coming together.

That said, my Inner Critic got irked often by shit he said. I couldn't **not** notice how often my Inner Critic got her buttons pushed by my bodybuilding boyfriend. This guy wasn't like anyone I had ever dated, overtly slapping my ass in semi-public areas for fun and getting upset if I turned him down for sex. Even when I was happy with how much progress I was making at the gym, somehow he found a way to make a new goal for us and make us feel like this progress didn't matter. I shrugged most of it off as encouraging criticisms. And yeah, we had a few conversations about dating other people and polyamory, but we decided to close our relationship a couple weeks ago. So when I found his phone wedged between the door and the passenger seat and saw what was on the screen, I realized that probably wasn't what he wanted at all.

There was absolutely no reason for him to have Tinder on his phone, and yet there it was. I was hopeful that my eyes were playing tricks as his phone battery died in my hands. No! I thought. I need to make sure that wasn't real. I plugged it into my car charger and started driving around the corners of the neighborhood to get the battery level to a point where I could turn it on again. Maybe I was imagining it. He wouldn't do that.... *would he?*

My Inner Critic got really vocal. *You just talked to him about how neither of you would do shit like this. What did you do to deserve this?* I didn't think I did anything, but I didn't realize that she wasn't asking me that question to blame me. It almost sounded like she was critiquing the situation as a whole, not me as an individual.

The college down the street had an empty parking lot. I glided into a parking spot and pressed his phone's ON button, hopeful that the notification was just my imagination. I swiped through his app list. Tinder was definitely there. I tapped the app open and saw a few messages from women, but not many. He seemed to message women and then switch to text as soon as possible.

My finger swiped towards his text messaging app, but my finger hovered over the screen for a moment. My Inner Critic took that moment to scold me. *Are you kidding me, Sam? You nosey, paranoid girlfriend. You're invading his privacy and turning into the very person you didn't ever want to be. What's wrong with you?*

I struggled with this for a moment. Was my Inner Critic right? I didn't know. I felt my resolve waver for a moment. *Am I* that nosey, paranoid girlfriend? I thought. My Inner Critic didn't skip a beat and tried to stop me. *Absolutely, yes! What the hell are you doing?* My insides felt tight, but it was a different type of tightness than when I believed her. This time, I wasn't sure if I did.

Have I been the nosey, paranoid girlfriend in the past? I asked myself. I tried to think of a few times, remembering some yelling and some insecure moments. I guess I have been. *No shit,* my Inner Critic said. But what about the opposite? Have there been times I've been the caring girlfriend that respects privacy? I thought through a few times, an image of calling his mother when she couldn't get a hold of him came to mind too, and then not answering her calls afterwards. I think I'm both?

My Inner Critic started wavering on her approach, and my hand was physically shaking a bit, still unsure if I was going to look at his text messages too. Finally, my finger shook enough to just hit the screen accidentally. That was when I saw the messages from his hometown friend, dated two days ago. He was bragging to his friend that he had slept with someone new two days in a row before seeing me that week.

My mind felt numb. I couldn't deny this one or make an excuse for him. It was right there. He's been cheating on me. My focus was on this message that revealed my greatest nightmare. And then it disappeared briefly as my eyes swelled up and dropped tears into my lap.

My Inner Critic began screeching at me. *Sam! This is all your fault!* She showed no mercy and reigned down on me. *How dare you not work harder to keep him! Of course he was bored with you and needed more action! If you just did more, had sex more, worked out more, ditched your friends to spend time with him more, you could have had it all with him! He would have never considered getting more with other women if you hadn't changed! I guess we're not good enough!*

I heard what she was saying, but this time felt different. It hurt, but not as deeply when she said these things before. Did I believe her? Was I really not good enough? I sat in my car, staring off into space with my mind flashing through memories of the past few months. The nights I gave up my plans to hang out with him. The afternoons I spent in the gym slogging through another free weights workout. The number on the scale going down steadily. Trying on a green dress at JC Penny's that was one size smaller than I wore before. I wasn't good enough? I thought I was good enough, considering everything I had done.

What if he's not good enough for us? I thought.

My Inner Critic paused. We reflected on the immature butt slapping in public, the heavy drinking on weeknights, the comments about our weight even now. She saw these images flash by, and she got small for a moment. Then suddenly I felt her rage flare back up as soon as she found a source to take her anger out on. What surprised me in this moment was that she didn't make *me* the source like she always had. Instead, my Inner Critic was enraged and ready to hurl some rocks. That asshole we thought was our loving boyfriend was her new target.

What the fuck have we been putting up with?! She raged. *We can do so much better than that! At least we can thank him for being a dick about us getting in shape so we can dump his ass while looking like the hot girl he can't have anymore.*

Weirdly enough, a rush of relief came over me. I felt calmer, seeing my Inner Critic redirect her energy at something even more worthy of criticizing. She was finally on board with me and wasn't attacking me for doing nothing wrong. Somehow, my Inner Critic was criticizing him. She was ready to take him down.

We only have an hour before he comes over, I thought. We need a plan.

She got giddy. *Oh, we've watched enough romantic comedies to know what to do. We know exactly how this is going down.* A few images flashed in my mind: he'd bang on the door to my house, not able to get in. He'd see me dressed in my black classic high heels and my flared skirt, my whole face done up to the nines. I'd hand him all the stuff he left at my house behind in a bag, his phone on top. He'd see his phone open on the text revealing his faux pas. When it finally registered with him that I caught him, I'd drive away to a bar with some friends that I've ignored far too much due to our relationship. I was impressed with her, but I also had to ask her something: you thought of everything, including protecting me from his criticisms. Why?

What do you mean, why? She asked, offended. *You're my numero uno. Everything I do is to protect you. Don't you know that yet?*

I laughed out loud. *You have a funny way of showing it*, I thought. I turned the ignition in my car. Before I went into gear, I took a picture of the texts revealing his crime with my own phone, about to send it to my best friend to explain what happened. "Yeah," I spoke out loud, "I'm done. Let's do this."

•••

Even while bedridden in my room in January 2019 I still smiled upon that memory fondly. *I'll never forget that day of smashing toxic masculinity in the face*, I thought to myself, smiling about how proud I was even two and a half years after. My favorite part was when I literally left him holding the bag – I had gathered all his stuff he left at my place – and drove off into the sunset right after I simply told him "Don't ever come back." I propped up my leg a little higher on the pillows, my knee swollen to the size of a children's soccer ball. I pressed the ice pack into my knee, wrapping a pillowcase around it to secure it. I winced a little before I reclined back and sighed, still reflecting on where I was right now. I went from epically breaking up with a cheater to epically snapping something in my knee in less than three years.

You idiot, my Inner Critic grumbled halfheartedly for the umpteenth time to me. *You knew you were in no shape for a trampoline. And good job for not being able to work for however long you're stuck like this.*

I giggled. At that point, I had been dealing with my Inner Critic for the five days my knee was swollen and painful. The first two days she came at me strong, telling me that I was stupid for going somewhere as dangerous as a trampoline park, selfish for demanding help from my boyfriend and friends, and on and on and on. But when she started making comments about how ugly my leg looked, it felt less like she was attacking me and more like she was being petty.

Of course my leg is hideous, I thought. *My knee is massive. My thigh is losing muscle mass. I haven't been able to shave it for a few days either. Nothing about this is supposed to be sexy.* I chuckled. *Seriously*, I thought. *You're the Eeyore to my Tigger.*

Someone's gotta be, my Inner Critic sneered. She was right. Without my Inner Critic, I might have had toxic and delusional optimism and injured myself more. I almost tried to walk on it the second day, but she screeched at me before I could do something like that. *Seriously, I'm glad your friend swung by with some crutches. Did you really think you could just walk this shit off?*

Yeah, not my finest idea, I admitted. *But I really didn't want to try to figure out how to navigate the kitchen.* One of my roommates was making living there hazardous. I had told both my roommates that I was getting around on crutches for the time being and needed the common spaces maintained to accommodate me. They both agreed, but one of them made no such attempt to make it easier for me. In fact, it almost seemed like he was making it worse for me *on purpose.*

I let my shoulders sink deeper into my bed. Just thinking about how I maneuvered around the kitchen minutes before just to get this fresh ice pack felt exhausting. To get to the kitchen refrigerator, I needed to gingerly hobble around on my borrowed, aluminum crutches through a daunting obstacle course of chairs, across the floor of the kitchen. Had the chairs been pushed into the table, this would have been no issue. Unfortunately for me, they managed to take up almost the entire square footage of the kitchen floor, making it impossible to see a straight path to the fridge on the other side of the entrance.

This is what you get for having cheap ass roommates, my Inner Critic pouted. *You get an asshole roommate that doesn't think about anyone but themselves.*

I felt tired listening to my Inner Critic go off about my inconsiderate roommate. I dreaded having to get up again in two hours to grab some dinner. I should have gotten it while I was up, but at least I pushed the chairs in this time.

Well, this is all your fault anyways, she reminded me. *You deserve to put up with this.*

What? I thought. Hearing that didn't feel funny this time. Thinking that I deserved to put up with a hazardous situation while seriously injured didn't make sense at all. *Do we deserve this? I think what we do deserve is a safe space to not worry about burdening other people.*

Clearly, asking your roommate to keep the kitchen clear for you is too much work for him, so how dare you burden him, she bickered bitterly. *And don't forget your friends, either. How much longer are you going to be relying on them for trips to the grocery store and anything else you need?*

I took that one in for a moment. Was I burdening them? That one felt more real. *Listen,* I tried to reason. *Any one of them could have said no while I'm figuring out what's going on with my knee, and I'm grateful they were able to help me.*

She wasn't convinced. She flashed an image of my boyfriend Noah coming back once again with a bag of food from the grocery store, tired and seemingly holding back on how annoyed he was that I was still relying on him. That felt real and painful.

Okay, you might be right, I admitted to my Inner Critic. I don't want that. We need to get out of this apartment.

Oh that's rich, she snorted. *Where do you expect us to go to get waited on while we're a sitting duck with our knee completely useless?*

A memory flashed through my mind from a few months ago to when my parents first moved into their new house. My mother had said, "If anything ever happens, we have an extra bedroom in this new house." My Inner Critic was frozen for a moment. She didn't know how to react for a moment. I was surprised at her silence.

You're not going to tell me that I'm giving up? I questioned her. You don't think that I'm letting myself get babied?

Of course I do, she snapped. Then she got quiet. *But your mom offered the help…*

She also used to work in a hospital, I reminded her. Plus she's retired now. In a new town on the beach in winter time. I do feel guilty about taking her up on it because I do want to be independent. But that's not something we can do right now, is it?

My Inner Critic fell silent, then gave in a bit more. *You're right*, she admitted. *I got nothing on that.* She seemed to mentally curl up and retreat. She seemed tired but felt taken care of. I was tired too. But I wouldn't feel taken care of until I got a yes. I searched my contacts and hit the call button.

"Hey mom, it's Sam. So you know how I have that doctor's appointment tomorrow? Is... is there any chance I can come home and stay with you for a bit while I'm recovering and figuring out what it is?"

Your Inner Critic has probably come out and said some shitty things to you while you've been by yourself during this period. Sometimes you probably believed it, sometimes it might have sounded ridiculous. Sometimes it might have been hard to tell what was truth and what was not. All of that insecurity is expected and normal. I wouldn't blame you if you wanted to destroy your Inner Critic for the mental and emotional bullshit they've slung at you. But your Inner Critic is also a permanent roommate, and they pay their rent by shining a light on your blindspots. Sometimes it's really painful to see them. However, your Inner Critic may be a roommate, but you're the live-in landlord. You get the final say on what you do in your house and how you think in your house, and you can absolutely try questioning them. Isn't it time that you start stepping into that power so you finally have the safe, loving home in your mind that you deserve? I think so.

Your Inner Critic probably wants that safe, loving home too. Their idea of what that looks like might be very different from what it actually is. When they bring something up that they don't like, it's your job to decide if it's worth taking care of or not. Just like when I pushed back and questioned my Inner Critic upon finding my ex's phone, you must begin to compassionately push back and question your Inner Critic when they are attacking your insecurities. If something they're saying doesn't seem right, ask them about it!

Make them slow down, pay attention, and realize they are not all-knowing. Tempering your Inner Critic's tirades against you can help them focus on criticising the *right* things. Inner Critics don't just criticize ourselves, but everything that seems like a threat to us. But as you start to show them when you're safe and don't need their input, they can start to focus energy on the RIGHT things to criticize.

Chapter 3: Journal Prompts

Think of some criticisms your Inner Critic loves to tell you. Write 2-3 strong ones below with the words "Am I" in front of the criticisms. E.g, if your criticism is "I'm dumb," instead write "Am I dumb?"

Now rewrite these criticisms in this form: "Have there been times when I…" After you write all of these questions down, read them out loud and think about them. Can you name a specific time that you have?

Now write the opposite of your criticisms in the space below with the words "Am I" in front of them. For example, if your criticism was "Am I dumb?" the opposite would be "Am I smart?"

Now rewrite these opposites in this form: "Have there been times when I…" After you write all of these questions down, read them out loud and think about them. Can you name a specific time that you have?

Look back at your "Have there been times when I..." questions. Is the answer "yes" for both the criticism *and* the matching opposite of any of your questions?

Rewrite your Inner Critic's message to one that matches what you see as true after looking at the opposites as well. They don't have to be the opposite answer, but it does need to be realistic. Using our previous example, one option could be "I'm smart, capable, AND I do dumb things sometimes."

We may not be able to uncover everything your Inner Critic yells at you, and some days your Inner Critic might do a good job beating you up. Luckily, even though you're stuck by yourself right now, you don't have to face your Inner Critic alone. These tools are your starting point to face your Inner Critic with curiosity and strength. Sometimes it's not always easy to do this yourself. While I'm not here to promote dependency on other people for your own self-confidence, asking others to help you question your Inner Critic from time to time can help you become self-confident. You can find the right people to support you in becoming self-confident even while you're isolated.

Chapter 4: From FOMO, ROMO, and Rethinking Socializing

I identify heavily as an extrovert, so when I first realized I was going to be away from all my friends for a long while during the recovery from my injury in 2019, I was depressed. FOMO, or *Fear of Missing Out,* was the first thing I thought I'd experience. I Imagined all my friends would be hanging out all the time without me. My mind went wild telling me they'd be going on overnight trips to Montreal, hosting biweekly pizza parties, watching movies together, going to karaoke bars, and exploring new places in the city… and they would be doing all of this without me. For a moment I even found myself worrying they might forget about me.

While the FOMO was something I was prepared for, I didn't expect the other thing that came up in my solitude – *Relief of Missing Out,* or "ROMO." I knew I would be missing awesome things that were happening as my friends' lives went on without me. But I also realized I wasn't going to miss the little nuances and stressors that came with being around my friends. For example, I wouldn't have to deal with seeing either of my exes at events. Thank God I wouldn't have to deal with that. Thank God I wouldn't have to rally myself up to go to the biweekly pizza parties and figure out who was hosting each week so I would know where to drive. Thank God I wouldn't have to worry about how I was going to afford one of the multi-day trips my friend group liked to organize periodically. Thank God I wouldn't have to embarrass myself for not knowing the latest tunes that people were singing at the karaoke bars. On top of all of this, I wouldn't be one of the few people that has a car and is always trying to navigate how to pick up my friends without cars and drive them to whatever function we're having. I didn't have to deal with any of those anymore while I was recovering.

It's not that I didn't enjoy the things I did with my friends – it's just that there were still stressors associated with doing them. I usually didn't notice these stressors because I was happy to be there and be a part of the fun. But while lounging on my parent's couch playing Candy Crush, I didn't feel the weight of what those social pressures did to me. I was finally off the hook for being constantly *on*. I didn't have to navigate awkward social interactions, comfort friends hurt by exes, or wear anything other than sweatpants. The work I typically put into showing up for my friends wasn't necessary in this situation, and I could put that work into healing from my injuries and caring for myself instead. Without all the people around me needing my attention, I felt comfortable swiping away incoming texts from group chats and close friends without answering them – knowing my injury was a good enough excuse to not respond. But after I had gotten my fill of time and space for myself, I noticed my desire to spend time with my friends starting to come back.

Before long, I started to feel lonely and forgotten more often. Sure, I had my mom to talk to about day-to-day things, and that helped feed my extroverted side. My physical therapist was also super friendly, and I could have upbeat little chats with her and the staff when I went to my sessions. I'd do one call with my life coach every other week, and I'd see my therapist the other weeks. My boyfriend would call me when he finished for the day, usually at some point after 9 p.m. And ironically, during the first two months of my recovery and isolation, I was teaching a virtual course on how to connect better as a professional cuddler! I should have been the last person to feel like I was disconnected and lonely given that I still had these outlets for connection, and yet I felt like I couldn't socialize the way I wanted to. I needed to have social interaction with my friends *somehow* or I'd be incredibly lonely and lose my mind.

Texting was a good place to start. Once I got through the backlog of texts I hadn't responded to, I realized I could talk to anyone on my phone – not just the people I saw nearly each week at home. I gave myself permission to reach out to whomever was in my phone contacts – from amicable past lovers, to old college friends, and people I met while I was traveling the summer before. I didn't engage them in heavy conversation right off the bat, but it felt nice to at least restart a conversation and let them know I was thinking of them. Even if I hadn't seen them in years, it was still nice to send them a message letting them know I care about them. I had the feeling that this was socially acceptable as opposed to calling them, emailing them or the likes. Some of these people I hadn't talked to in years asked how I was, and I'd tell them I was injured and we'd talk about that. The responses, updates, condolences, and well wishes I got in return made me feel a little less alone for a while.

One morning, I woke up to a *really* long text message first thing in the morning from a friend. I'm talking about *six or seven paragraphs in one text.* And there were multiple texts. They took up the entire screen, and I had to scroll to get to the bottom of four monster-sized texts. It was a heavy, emotionally-charged text about her boyfriend and how he was being so aloof she felt ignored and suspicious of him. She divulged all these deep insecurities around the situation. I felt bad for her as I skimmed the message, but I also noticed that I suddenly didn't feel as well-rested as I did moments before. I could feel the exhaustion from emotionally processing what she was telling me set in. *This is not something I can respond to first thing this morning,* I thought. Instead of reading it line by line and responding, I swiped the message away to do something else on my phone.

I felt guilty when I realized I didn't want to read it. It wasn't that I didn't care about what she had to say. I actually *did* want to know about what was going on and support her! Even so, in that moment I realized something really important about how I use text messages: *I don't like getting play-by-play stories, long explanations, or intense emotions via text without warning.* When I open my phone to send a text, I want to have short conversations and not expect a quick answer back. When I was younger, I was used to sending and receiving long texts. As I got older, I realized maybe I needed to use something other than text if sending my friends something will require them to scroll several times.

After having taken some time mostly off from texting, I began to notice how much better I felt hearing or seeing someone in person as opposed to texting back and forth with them extensively. I realized being in person brought the deeper conversations I had with friends *even* deeper. But there needed to be another way to get that fix if I couldn't physically have them in front of me. That's when one of my friends asked if we could video chat about some productivity tools I was asking him about. I agreed, and we got on a Zoom video call. On the call, he explained to me how the productivity system I was interested in worked and how it differs from what he uses. He shared his computer screen, waved his hands around, and overall was entertaining to watch on screen.

Near the end of his explanation, he started trailing off in his own thoughts. "It does require a little bit of accountability, and I haven't been doing this weekly review in a while," he murmured.

I perked up and asked him, "Do you want an accountability buddy then?" He widened his eyes and nodded vigorously. From there, we began meeting once and sometimes twice a week to talk about what we were working on and what was going on in our lives via video chat.

At first, these video chats felt great to do. I got to see my friend on video, he could share his screen with me when he was talking about something he wanted to reference, and I could see his animated facial expressions that sometimes mimicked a cartoon character. As time went on however, I realized I got physically and mentally tired on videochat quickly. My attention was on the screen and whatever my friend had to say, but it was also split with looking at myself and making sure that I looked like I was paying close enough attention. On top of that, it was still really hard to read body language when I wasn't physically with a person. I found myself subconsciously and automatically looking for body language on his video that I couldn't find, which was what was wearing me out fast. I started to dread doing video chats, knowing that I would feel that way by the end of the calls.

After a couple of days of reflecting on my new realization, I began to think of an alternative. I realized, one of my favorite ways to connect from a distance was regular phone calls. It happened when I was on the phone with my boyfriend, Noah for our nightly chat before bed. My leg was strong enough that I could start pacing a little around the room, so I stood up and started making little figure eights on the dark hardwood floor in the bedroom where I was staying. He told me about his improv class and the latest melodramas at his theater. I talked about the new training I started at physical therapy and some new recipes my mom had shared with me. We began to make plans for him to come visit after my surgery for a weekend, and I asked him to bring something to do while he was down here because I would be a pretty boring person in recovery. The conversation had no real objective, we just wanted to hear from each other and feel connected.

I realized how natural it felt to be on the phone, compared to texting and video chat. I was surprised how easy it was for me to keep conversation flowing with him despite brushing my hair, taking my bra off, and even doing a few leg exercises while chatting with him. Noah was none the wiser about it because I was still paying attention and listening despite the background multitasking.

At first I attributed my comfort level in this conversation to the fact that it was with Noah – and of course, I was more comfortable with him than most people. But then I got a call from my friend Peter, and then another from my friend Corwin. Then I got a call from my friend Ann, and then another from Will. Then Matt asked for help via text, and I talked with him on the phone too. Each time someone called, I felt natural about picking up the phone and talking. I felt completely at ease on the phone, found myself trying to pace a bit, and I was absorbed in the conversation. After each call, I felt better than I did when I started. What made phone calls so easy but video chats and texts not so much?

I began to realize it was what I *didn't* have to do when on a phone call that made it so easy for me. When I was only hearing someone's voice (as opposed to seeing them or reading their words), I didn't have to be on a video screen and appear engaged in conversation. I didn't have to worry about the lighting. I didn't have to be obvious in how I expressed myself. In fact, I didn't even have to be sitting up. On top of that, I didn't need to re-read words on a screen to make sure I understood them correctly before I responded. Being on a phone call gave me enough feedback with intonation, emotion, speed of absorbing information, and responding in real time – without straining to read body language or worrying how I looked while talking. While the other ways of communicating were nice and helped a lot, I preferred phone calls so much more.

If you're isolating right now and have to be more of a hermit than usual, that doesn't mean you have to live under a rock the whole time. Here's a reframe: **this time in isolation is giving you the opportunity to press the reset button on all of your connections and rethink how you socialize and interact with them.** In fact, it may even be easier to create *better* connections while you're physically away from everyone, because you're not forced to be in their immediate vicinity. You, like me, might realize you *really fucking dread* scrolling to read the long-ass text you got out of the blue filled with a detailed, emotional story. Or, you might discover the exact opposite about yourself! The point is, right now is a great time to be intentional about who you connect with and how. Take this time to explore what mediums you prefer to connect through and which connections feel best. Not everyone will be like me and want to do phone calls. In fact, there's a lot of in-between options that are available to connect even more briefly, like video messages, voice clips, topic-based group threads, and more. There are also some more "old school" methods like email, snail mail, or even just seeing if someone wants to drop by briefly. Now is a particularly good time to start getting familiar with which communication modalities work best for you and with whom you want to share those connections.

Chapter 4: Journal Prompts

When you're not hermitting, what do you use to talk to people? Include apps, sites, social media, etc.

What have you been using while you've been hermitting to talk to or interact with people? Do the same as above and include apps, sites, social media, etc.

Of the two lists above of tools you've been using, circle the ones you use the most. Put a star next to the ones you feel best using the most when you use them. If something is both, circle it and put a star next to it. Rewrite those tools below.

For each of your circled and starred items, think of a time when you realized you needed to step away from a conversation on that platform or needed to stop using the tool altogether. How will you be able to stop that again before you get too tired or emotionally spent from using the tool? What will you do instead of use that tool? This could include turning off your phone, going for a walk, cooking without your phone, etc. Name a few ideas for yourself.

Figuring out what you want to use to communicate with your friends is a great starting point. But ultimately, you also need to find the *people* that will be in your corner to talk to using these tools as well and how you'll talk to each other. In the next chapter, we talk about the different roles you'll need others to be in your life to help you stay connected and be a happier hermit and even happier post-hermitting.

Chapter 5: Your Core 4 and Why You Need Them

For most of my twenties, I didn't know I was leaning too hard on some of my friends and romantic partners for emotional support they didn't sign up to give. I didn't realize I was pushing them to the edge of their emotional capacity by sharing all of my heavy emotions unabashed, day after day. The worst part was, many of my friends and my exes didn't even realize themselves that this was why they naturally started avoiding me after a while. This meant I wasn't able to adjust my behavior in other relationships because I wasn't getting the feedback I needed to change. If I was able to get any feedback from them before they disappeared, it was often along the lines of "I can't keep up with you." I would assume they just couldn't handle my intensity, and I'd get defiant and self-righteous about the ending of our relationship.

I was especially guilty of doing this in my romantic relationships. I would begin to solely rely on my significant others for all my emotional needs and not lean on my friends at all until we would break up. It was a whole cycle: Have great friendships. Meet new boyfriend. Get really attached to new boyfriend. Share a metric shitton of emotional stuff with them daily. Get deeper in our relationship. Completely forget about all of my friends. Only share everything with my boyfriend. They reach their breaking point. Get confused because I did nothing different than before. Get resistant or distant. Break up. Crawl back to friends I ignored. Rinse and repeat. It wasn't until one night during my recovery when my boyfriend Noah (whom I had been dating for less than a year at that point) stood up to me and asked me to stop doing this to him. Instead of repeating my typical cycle of emotionally overloading my boyfriend, he helped me break it and as a result, I discovered a new way of looking at my relationships.

...

I had been calling Noah at the end of nearly every day in February 2017. I noticed I was getting into a habit of griping to him about my parents' lives and my own struggles with recovery, but he was willing to listen and was generally supportive. This one Thursday was a little different though. It was near the end of February and just two weeks before my ACL surgery. I was trying to keep my voice low enough for my parents to not hear my words through the thin walls of the first floor bedroom. The living room was just a few feet away from the bedroom door, so it would be easy for them to hear my tearful voice and simply put their ear to the door to hear what I was saying. My parents had tried to eavesdrop on my intimate conversations since I was a teenager, and this new house made maintaining privacy harder.

I felt angry about what had happened earlier after dinner with my dad. Telling Noah what happened always made me feel better, so I normally never held back on sharing what I was feeling, especially as it related to my parents. It did feel like I had more to say about my parents than usual, but he seemed okay with me talking about these high-strung feelings that come up around interacting with my parents.

This particular day's high-strung emotions involved my dad sitting tight-lipped while my mom answered my question about how they managed their money. I wanted to work on my own money management and do better in this area than I had been doing before my injury, and I was looking for advice from them. I knew my dad had a lot to say about money management because he had never held back on that topic before, but tonight he was sitting in silence. To prompt him to contribute to the conversation, I turned to him when my mom took a break from talking and asked him if he could add anything. He replied curtly that he just does whatever my mom tells him to do. I had expected more from him, but this passive aggressive comment was all he offered us. I looked over at my mom and her face fell. I felt my blood freeze at his icy response. When he stormed off from the kitchen table and upstairs without a word after his cutting response, I felt my head spin, trying to figure out what the *hell* just happened.

I went to my room and leaned back in my bed with my leg propped up, feeling my face get warm and my eyes get watery. My mom didn't do anything wrong, so why was my dad treating her that way? Or was that meant to be directed at *me*? What was he holding back and why? I felt so confused and was trying to process this with Noah out loud. I was hearing my own voice start to really waver when Noah finally stopped me. I paused. He took a deep breath in and slowly said, "Sam, I... I can't keep this up."

My heart dropped to my stomach and my shoulders tensed. I knew those words too well, and I knew what that usually meant. My Inner Critic started crying out that I wasn't good enough, once again, that he had definitely had enough of my bullshit and was finally cutting the cord. I sat frozen for a few more seconds as my head whirred. *Was he really breaking up with me?* I thought. *In the middle of my ACL recovery? Was this conversation the straw that broke the camel's back?* I needed him to be here for me right now in this super trying time. Was he really going to walk away now?

He continued, my swimming mind trying to process what he might say next. "I love you. I'm just tired and can't hold all of these heavy emotions you're handling right now." He said.

I felt my heart do a strange flip in my stomach for a moment. I was confused. "Wait, so you're not breaking up with me?"

"What? No!" he exclaimed. "Sam, no of course not."

My shoulders relaxed and I sighed out a breath I didn't even realize I was holding in. "Okay," I whispered. "So what are you telling me then?"

"Sam," he started, "I'm dealing with a lot at the improv theater right now. Work's been more busy than it was when you were here before. I want to hear about these things and be there for you, but it's a lot to do when I'm dealing with my own stuff too."

That totally made sense. I didn't know why, but hearing him tell me that made me realize that I too would often check out of heavy conversations like this when I had a lot on my plate. It didn't mean I cared any less and I didn't want that person to open up to me, but I needed some time not hearing about it. It's draining even just to listen to heavy emotional stuff.

"Thank you for telling me," I slowly responded. "I guess I need to talk with a few of my friends more about this."

"Sam," Noah started. "I don't want you to not tell me these things. I want to be there for you when you tell me about these things. But I can't do that when I'm distracted. I feel guilty when I can't do that for you."

Oh! I thought. He thinks that he's robbing me because he can't show up how he wants to? "Please don't feel guilty," I said. "I'm the one putting these things on you without warning. If I have someone else to talk to about this, will you be upset if I don't always talk to you extensively about these things?"

I could practically feel the relief he exuded over the phone. "Of course I won't be upset, Sam." He said. "I want you to be happy."

"Can you listen as I talk through who I might be able to talk to other than you?" I asked him.

"Of course!" he said without hesitating.

For the next ten minutes I talked with Noah, mostly one-sided, about various friends I could talk to, what I should talk about with my therapist, and what to cover with my life coach. We even touched upon what to share with my mom and what support I could get from her. He made a few comments about friends he'd met that he thought would be good supports for talking about certain things but not others, and he affirmed some suspicions I had that I couldn't go super deep with some friends yet, seeing where we were with our friendship. By the end of those ten minutes, I felt more solid in our relationship and like I had a support network. Noah felt relieved and like he could have a better idea of what to expect from me.

"One more thing Noah," I called out before Noah could hang up. "I just wanted to ask you one more thing. Can I trust you to tell me when it's too much for you? I don't want to overburden you and resent me for what I give you."

"Oh, Sam," he cooed sweetly. "Of course. I love you."

After I hung up, I grabbed a pen and paper so I could write my thoughts down a bit. "Who can I talk to about things when I can't talk with Noah?" I thought out loud, writing it down on the piece of paper. I began thinking through the summary of our conversation and the names of a few people I wanted to talk to more to take the emotional burden off of Noah. I looked over the list of people I had and realized that I wouldn't have the same conversation with any one of these people, but that was exactly why I needed to have conversations with *all of these people.* Each person had a different way of giving attention and being there for me, and that was the beauty of it!

I began comparing some of my friends' strengths in certain areas and the type of support they would normally give. One friend was good at dissecting sticky problems for solutions. One friend was usually dealing with similar feelings as me, and we'd work together on them and update each other. One friend loved cheering for me when I did something great and it was super satisfying to get their praise. One friend was incredibly impressive and I looked up to them in how put together their life was. One friend was a thoughtful giver and, if I opened up to them, would usually be proactive in checking in on me even before I asked for help. One friend was a really good listener. While I could share the same things with different friends, this exercise helped me realize that I had friends that were good at giving in different ways, and Noah was no different. The way he gave to me was going to be different than another friend, and forcing him to take on a different role than what he's good at every day was going to exhaust him. I realized that these roles my friends – and I – can take on for others were the starting point for me developing the acronym I call the CORE4.

It's really easy to lean on someone you care about when you're away from everyone else, but that doesn't mean you should. If you insist on talking with the one contact you have about every single problem, thought, or topic – you might risk losing that one connection. In the same way I realized I was putting unwanted pressure on my boyfriend to show up for me while recovering from my injury, I want you to realize that you can release your loved ones from that pressure as well. I'm going to break down the acronym I call CORE4, describe each role, and help you consider how to get your needs met in each of these areas. This can help mitigate unwanted pressure on anyone in your life while you're in isolation.

I want you to keep in mind that CORE4 only highlights different support roles people can take on. These roles can be taken on and off. Taking on these roles doesn't mean that any one person is expected to do this all the time. On the other hand, if someone makes an honest attempt at filling that role and it doesn't help you, that doesn't mean they are a bad friend or not worth keeping a relationship with. They're just doing the best they can with their own limited knowledge. The better you can ask for what you want from the people filling your CORE4 roles, the more likely they'll be able to give to you the way that you want them to. Otherwise, the support you'd receive from them is simply their best guess at what they think someone would want in this situation, and that's not always a reliable way to operate. While some of these roles may come naturally to you or certain friends, there is nothing wrong with asking for exactly what you need from someone.

On the flip side of that, you can ask your friends what kind of support *they* want too. When you take on a CORE4 role for someone else, asking them what they want from you can help guide your friends to ask for what they really want too. However, leaving that question open-ended like "How can I support you?" creates more work for your friend. My friend Mark Boughton from Authentic Revolution summarizes the types of support you can offer succinctly: what kind of box do you need? Do you need a soapbox, a tissue box, or a toolbox? CORE4 has creative ways to offer all three of these boxes in this role.

C is for Celebrate

The C in CORE 4 is people you can celebrate with. When you think of celebrating, you might think of sharing and applauding good news, like a new job or a baby. But celebrating isn't limited to just big news. We can celebrate exercising, cooking a full meal for ourselves, being productive at work today, or even staying within our budgets. Think of this as celebrating the small wins and having someone positive in your corner that you can share your happiness with.

C people tend to be very positive people no matter what kind of support they are offering in any given situation. Standing your ground on your soapbox in a heated debate? C people are the ones that cheer you on while you're tearing your opponent to shreds. Lost your job and feel like garbage? C people's version of a tissue box is appreciating the positive parts of you while you pour your heart out about getting let go. Struggling to figure out how to fit your workouts in the next week? C people remind you of how powerful you are, and remind you that you've figured out hard things like this before. People in this role might not always help you solve your problems directly, but they're amazing at empowering you with positivity so you can move forward.

However, the dark side of empowerment and positivity can show up as insensitivity and delusion. Being empowering is *not* the same as being positive no matter what. Shining a light in dark situations isn't a bad thing, but positivity unbridled can turn into *toxic positivity*. An extreme example of this would be if I told you my grandmother died, and you responded with, "But you have another grandmother that's alive and well! And you're alive and well too, aren't you? That's something to be happy about! No tears today, just think happy thoughts."

I (and most sane people) would want to slap the shit out of you for being so insensitive if you said that. But smaller, microaggressive versions of this scenario happen all the time. If it's not trying to think positive about the fact your grandmother died, it might be a friend cutting you off from talking about your bad day so they can tell you how great something else is. If you've ever wondered why you're irritated with your good-natured, positive friend, this might be exactly why. Oftentimes C people get uncomfortable seeing people unhappy and feel it's their job to make it better. Telling a C person that overly positive support isn't what you want or need right in that moment can be disorienting for someone so used to operating in positive thinking no matter what. At times, it's also exactly what these people need to hear. This feedback and new awareness might help them adjust to a healthier C-person way of showing up, or it might even help them switch to a different role when it's appropriate.

On a broad level, social media is really good for finding lots of people to celebrate your wins with. If you're looking for a friend to celebrate something specific, think of the things that you care about and you'd naturally want to share with someone. It usually makes sense to celebrate specific accomplishments, events, or moments with people who would be easy to share this with, and who you think would be excited for you. There might be group chats or specific friends who would love to hear about your exercise wins, and others who would prefer you keep those to yourself. If someone is struggling in the area you're celebrating, they might feel jealous and resentful instead, so be wary of sharing wins with those struggling. The best way to figure out the right C people in a given situation is simply to ask if you can share your wins on a particular topic and see how they respond.

Chapter 5: C Journal Prompt

Who do you know that's a great celebrator? Write their names down and next to them, things you have celebrated or would like to celebrate with them.

How are you a great celebrator? Jot down a few times you've celebrated others outwardly and openly and how you want to so moving forward.

O is for Open Up To

The O in CORE 4 is people you can Open Up To. When you think of this, you might be thinking of 4am talks with a friend at a party when everyone gets really vulnerable. The 4am shares at a party is what I live for – but opening up isn't limited to those big shares. It can also be opening up about how you're feeling about your day-to-day life. Your version of opening up can be as small as being the target of some road rage from a driver on your way to work and admitting that you're feeling insecure about driving through rotaries. It can also be as big as sharing that your boss might be making more budget cuts, and that you're feeling nervous about being laid off. Think of O people as the people you can share just about anything with, and they don't judge you for telling them.

O people have more flexible offerings than C people when it comes to the type of box they can give you. They can hold space for you while you're on your soapbox ranting, raving, crying, or being pissed at everything. Really strong O people have the emotional awareness to not take responsibility for your big emotions when you share them. They can also listen and comfort you while you let out your emotions as their version of a tissue box. Sometimes they might even give you a literal tissue box! The toolbox O people can offer you might be one of two possibilities: either silent support or thoughtful responses. Silent support is simply giving you focused attention in silence. This type of toolbox can give you space for you to emotionally and mentally process what you share for them while they observe you. Thoughtful responses might look like asking questions so they can understand where you're coming from and be there for you more. Both toolboxes O people can give you empower you to realize the solution for yourself, rather than them giving you the solution. In my opinion, O people's way of giving support is one of the most essential roles in the CORE4.

O people are understanding, accommodating, and kind. They often feel very deeply for you about what you share with them. However, the support they offer is often discounted because what they do isn't easily pointed to as a solution. As a result, an O person is often the underappreciated O person for many people at the same time. They may hold space so often that they reach a point where they feel physically and emotionally exhausted. This is often referred to as compassion fatigue, and it's also why most people get depressed when they watch the news too often. O people without boundaries are less likely to stop you from sharing your emotions out of fear of seeming heartless. If they feel forced to take on the emotional labor of processing their feelings around your shares while holding space for you, they might start to resent you. Like Noah taught me in our conversation that evening, not everyone is able to do this role as well and as often as we'd like them to due to compassion fatigue. It helps a lot to check in with someone before sharing by saying "Do you have the space for me to share a big emotional thing that happened today with you?" This can prime an O person to step into that role or decide that they can't be there for you in that moment as well as they want to.

Asking if they are open to hearing an emotional thing is also a good way to test the waters with someone new you might meet that you think might be a good O person for you. In my experience, most people welcome being opened up to. Talking about something deeper than the weather or traffic subconsciously gives permission to others to open up to you in return. This invites deeper conversations and connections. However, an emotionally aware O person will listen and not feel compelled to fix your problems. This is less common to find, but once you're able to find someone who's willing and able to simply listen and not tell you what to do, you'll have an amazing support for life.

Chapter 5: O Journal Prompt

Who do you know that's a great Open Up To person? Write their names down and next to them things you have or would like to open up to them about.

How are you a great Open Up To Person? Jot down a few times you've let others open up to you and how you want to show up for that moving forward.

R is for Respect

The R in CORE 4 is Respect, otherwise known as look up to. This is someone that is doing things the way you want to do them, is inspiring, gives helpful advice, or overall is a role model. Your first thoughts might be a coach or therapist, a boss or executive in your company, a leader in your industry that you personally know, or even an older relative. All of those people may give great advice or be people you respect, and they may be an R person for you, but an R person doesn't have to fit into one of these very official positions and limiting relationships. An R person that you can have a personal and intimate friendship or relationship with might be your awe-inspiring romantic partner or your badass entrepreneur friend. It could be that person that was a year ahead of you in school that you hang out with and they seem to just have all their shit together. They might not be doing exactly what you want to be doing, but they may do or teach things you aspire to emulate in your own life.

Much like O people, they may also be someone you confide in and open up to, but there's a distinct difference in how R people show up for you when you open up to them. When you share with them and want to be on a soapbox, they may smile and be proud of you for speaking up. When you need a tissue box, they may share their own experiences and struggles in similar situations. When you need a toolbox, they can give you some solutions that have worked for them or point you in a direction to start looking. They may coach you, give you advice, or give you a resource. In order to get this kind of support, ask them questions on how they would do something. Ask them if you can call on them for help. Respecters can be valuable people that help you find direction when you're not sure where to go and grounding when you need support.

At times, R people can take their position too far and, ironically, lose your respect for them. One big problem R people run into is giving unsolicited advice when they see a problem. R people without boundaries tend to overfunction as problem-solvers even when no one's asking them to solve a problem. They might also steal your conversation and attention by sharing their own story. Sometimes this is welcome, but unhealthy R people will do this constantly to make a point and share a lesson while thinking they're "relating" to you. They don't always realize they're annoying the shit out of their friends and they'd be better off shutting up and listening to them instead of unintentionally stealing the limelight. When left unchecked, these oversharing of related personal stories can cause you to resent your R person instead of feel good around them. To combat this, most R people will respond well to being appreciated for the intention behind their actions *and then* being told that it's not helpful right now. That might sound like this: "I appreciate that you want to help me solve my problem by giving me solutions, but can you give those to me later when I ask for them? Right now I think I need xyz instead."

To find an R person to look to, first consider some of the people you already have in your life. Siblings, cousins, neighbors and roommates might be able to fill the role of R person for you. You might have a friend you're not super close to yet, but you value that they really have their shit together and want to be more like them. An R person isn't necessarily perfect in every way you want to be, but they might be really grounded in one aspect of their life you admire.

Chapter 5: R Journal Prompt

Who do you know that's a great Respecter? Write their names down and if they're a professional or a personal contact.

How are you a great Respecter? Jot down a few times you've been the person people respect and how you want to show up for that moving forward.

E is for Elevate

The E in CORE 4 is Elevate, otherwise known as grow. Think of this as someone in the trenches with you working on the same goals, projects, or struggles that you are. People in this role might be accountability buddies, coworkers in a same or similar role, classmates, or friends with similar interests. They might be slightly further along with something you're looking to do, be, or improve. They also might be a little further behind than you. Elevators are really great for just about anything you're looking to improve and have accountability for. With an E person, you're on similar playing fields and you're pushing each other to do better.

The way an E person supports you might look a lot like how some of the other roles support you, but it is actually vastly different. They might cheer for you while you're on your soapbox, but they are on theirs at the same time. They might comfort you when you need a tissue box, but they're also trying to help you through it so you can both keep going. They might be giving solutions to you while you're looking for a toolbox, but they're also brainstorming solutions with you so they can move forward together. E people are there for you and they want you to grow with them. Their support might look a lot like many other CORE4's roles, but it's marked with an intention to learn, grow, and be your best selves past those moments of support.

E people's way of offering support is a delicate balance between encouraging and damaging. As a result, there's a ton of ways this type of relationship can turn shitty really fast. Because they are more likely to relate to what you need support on, they are also at risk of either trying to gloss over the fact that there's a problem or they may dig into the problem and ruminate on it longer than you want to. An unhealthy E person might also look down on a problem and belittle your woes as a way to "encourage" you. Lastly, if one of you pulls way ahead of the other, E people can get really insecure about their position and start being passive aggressive with you. To avoid this shitstorm, create more structure to conversations and agree to talk about progress regularly. This might sound like this: "Can we agree that when we talk about our projects, we'll talk about successes to celebrate, failures to grieve, and then ask questions to help us brainstorm how to move forward? I'd like that for myself, and I want to be there for you in that way too if you want that since you're my accountability buddy here." That alone can go far to assuage any insecurities that might arise from successes or failures.

To find a great E person, think about something you want to improve on while in isolation right now. This can be fitness goals, learning something new, progress at work on projects, career advancement, personal projects, and more. Who do you know that also wants to improve on this? The upside is if the answer is no one, that's okay. You can also look in relevant social media groups you're already a part of. There, you can ask if there's anyone else working on something similar and if they'd want an accountability buddy. If you do this, I recommend doing a video chat with the person before committing. E people will take work to organize, but they are able to empower you in a way that the other CORE4 can't because E people are in the trenches with you.

Chapter 5: E Journal Prompt

What do you want to improve in your life?

Who do you know that's a great Elevator for this? Write their names down. If you can't think of any, write down where you can go to find them.

How can you ask them for support? Write down the words that you'll use when you reach out to them.

Adding each of these roles into your life and social circle requires you to actively seek out these relationships and intentionally shape them. You may find them in your current friend groups, through professional contacts, or common interests. However you find them, you need to communicate better in order to have healthier dynamics in whatever CORE4 role you need or want to be in your life.

Chapter 6: Minimize Your Closet, Not Other People's Feelings

I glided up the ramp to the orthopedics' office on my crutches in February 2019. I had been using them for three weeks and my mom was surprised at how adept I got to using them as we checked in at the front desk. I didn't take in these compliments she gave me while we waited for the doctor to come in. At that point, three weeks felt really long and I was ready to be told what to do next. My knee was still aching and swollen with an ace bandage tightly wrapped around it.

Despite all of this pain and uncertainty, I was beginning to feel positive about this whole situation with my knee. I expected the MRI I had last week to show that I tore my meniscus, the little cartilage by the knee joints. Everything I was reading online about my knee pointed to having that injury. Based on my research, depending on what kind of tear it was, I might not even need all that invasive of a surgery. There was a possibility that I would be fine and moving around in six to eight weeks easily, and if they simply removed the tear instead of repairing it, I'd be able to walk again immediately after the procedure. It would be simple. I would be fine. This was the assumption and attitude I entered the appointment with, which is why when I met the surgeon and he unceremoniously broke the news that my MRI indicated a full-on ACL tear and it would take me a year to recover after surgery, I was suddenly NOT fine.

I was also no stranger to what ACL injuries looked like. My older sister had torn both of her ACL's, one in high school, and one for a second time in college. I saw her frustrations with recovering, how painful it was for her at night, and how helpless she was during that time to do anything. In the moment when the surgeon broke the news to me, I heard my parents' comments about her and her sudden sluggishness for months after the surgery echoing in my head, knowing now that this might be my reality in the near future too. Even today, my sister's knees ache whenever it's about to rain due to the air pressure, and she didn't play soccer quite the same way for a long time after her injuries. Picturing all of this and being faced with my stoic surgeon, I felt my eyes beginning to water.

The doctor paid no attention to my sudden shock and continued delivering information about the surgery I would need to move forward. He told me I would need to do preoperative physical therapy for a month to strengthen the leg before surgery would be possible. He stressed the importance of getting my leg strengthened enough to keep my knee perfectly straight so they could operate on it properly. I nodded passively while he confidently mentioned that preoperative physical therapy would have me ready for surgery one month from now. When my mom suggested that I would do physical therapy down by their place instead of in Boston, he told us that I would need an out-of-network referral to see a physical therapist in Cape Cod. He said I would be at full strength in a year, but I could recover quickly enough in six months to resume most physical activities without a brace on. I'd need a brace for at least four months.

As the doctor who was now my surgeon rattled on with his tone deaf info dump of expectations, I was staring off into the human diagram of joints and muscles on the wall in front of me, trying not to blink for fear of my tears spilling. I was still feeling frozen from shock. My mind kept flashing back to memories of my sister crying, frustrated with her knee brace on while trying to run like she used to on the soccer field. This was going to be my life now. Even after I recovered, my physical abilities might never be the same again. And I was only twenty eight years old, an age I had thought of to be one of the last prime years I had for physical ability. *My life is never going to be the same*, I kept thinking over and over again. I felt very alone in the doctor's office with my silent mom and my stoic and emotionless surgeon. I wanted nothing more than to get out of this clinic as fast as possible so I could cry.

Ten excruciatingly long minutes later, I was booking it out of the hospital on my crutches and heading home with my mom. That was ten minutes longer than I had wanted to sit in this office, but the front desk needed to handle some paperwork for us before we left. More news and realizations began hitting me as I thrust my crutches in front of me as fast as I could. I wouldn't be able to move back to my apartment for at least two months. My thigh muscles had already shrunk from melon-sized to apple sized from not using my leg since the injury. I couldn't believe that I was expected to strengthen them for a month just so they could shrink again after surgery. It would take a year for my muscles to come back in my leg. I wouldn't be able to consider any activity other than walking until three months after surgery, when I would finally have some of the muscle back. "Any activity" included dancing. One of my favorite ways of expressing myself was off the table for at least another three months.

Even then, it would be a struggle with all the scar tissue I would likely have in my knee.

We left the appointment, I finally lowered myself into the car, and my mom put the keys in the ignition. Knowing that I would not be able to do what I wanted to physically do felt so heavy and restricting in that moment. My chest tightened as I closed the passenger door to the car and my eyes blurred with tears desperately wanting to spill. I finally couldn't hold any of this massive weight in me anymore and let out a small yelp. I was heartbroken. This was my life now. Even after I recovered, my physical abilities might never be the same again. It seemed I was going to be forced to waste one of my last youthful years recovering from an injury. I started shedding silent tears.

My mom didn't notice my grieving while we drove over to the grocery store. She started talking out loud about what she was planning to get at the store, but I wasn't really listening. Once she parked, she turned to me and asked what I wanted from inside. I stared blankly ahead, not looking at her and still crying silently. How could I bring myself to think about groceries when I just found out that my entire year, possibly my entire life, was going to be upended by this injury?

My mom finally noticed the red on my face and the tears streaming down my cheeks. "What, are you still upset?" My mom asked, confused.

I turned to her incredulously, tears dripping down my face. "Mom, I *just* found out about this ten minutes ago."

"Well, there's no changing it, so getting upset about it won't make it better. Now, do you want clementines?" She said in a positive and upbeat tone.

Even though the words she said were different, my mind filled in so many blanks with how to interpret them. *Stab.* It felt like she took needles to my heart with those words. *Stab stab.* It felt like my thoughts and worries didn't matter. *Stab, stab, stab.* She might as well have said "Whatever, the past is the past, stay positive about this now." *Staaab.* I felt belittled for grieving. I had no idea what to even say to something that seemed so insensitive.

I drudged along with my mom's wishes, taking to my phone in the car as a distraction while I waited for her to do the grocery shopping. I tried to forget about my newfound dependence. After leaving the store, we went back to my apartment to pick up more of my belongings. My parents had just moved to their new house on the Cape a year before and I no longer had many personal belongings there, so I would need to bring more clothes and other comfort items to help me feel more at home there. My mom also decided she would clean some spaces in my apartment before we left, so she spent some time in my kitchen and living room working by herself.

While my mom was in the common spaces, I worked in the bedroom. I gloomily piled items on my bed that I would need at her house. Since I couldn't bend over or grab items on the floor easily, I mindlessly tossed them from my dresser and my desk onto my bed. My mind began to wander to what my life might look like now. *When will the next time I sleep in this bed be? I'll still be paying rent on this place while I'm gone. I'm definitely coming back, but I won't be able to visit my friends. Most of them don't have cars either, so they probably won't come see me. Will I even be able to drive my car? Possibly, once I can sit in the car comfortably with my knee, but who knows when that might be.* While I dwelled on these answers, it really dawned on me that I was about to be completely reliant on my parents for even the most basic things, like eating, for a few *months*. I felt so depressed and defeated. My shoulders felt heavier at this realization and my whole body wanted to slump into my piles of belongings on the bed.

My mom came into my room with a rag and some dusting agent in her hands. She saw me with my head lowered, picking up items and moving them from one pile to another emotionlessly. "When are you going to stop being upset about this?" She snapped, now seeming condescending that I was still depressed about my situation.

Just over an hour had passed since I began grieving the temporary loss of my independence, my physical ability, and my personal life as I had built it over the past six years. Hearing my mom ask this, I did stop being sad for a moment, but it wasn't to be chipper and happy like she was asking of me. Instead, I felt an angry fire spark in my chest and throat, and I needed to unleash it.

"When will *you* let me feel my feelings?" I snapped at her. I gave her an icy cold look as I felt hot tears form in my eyes. "Seriously, anyone would be upset about this! Why can't I just be sad and upset right now?" I was finally not having it. My ACL wasn't the only thing hurting right now. If she was going to try to ignore that and minimize my emotional pain, I was going to show her how real and huge it was. I was ready to defend my feelings and let them heal at their own pace, even if it meant taking the offensive to do it.

She didn't have anything to say to that and backed out of the room, continuing to clean the living room spaces silently. We had a pretty silent 90 minute ride back to her house while I stewed in frustration and grief. Both of us were uncomfortable with this whole exchange. Looking back, I realize she had good intentions but ultimately, painful effects. She loved (and still loves) me, and she didn't want me to suffer or be uncomfortable. She was uncomfortable with seeing me uncomfortable, but that projection of wanting to comfort me when I didn't need the type of comfort she gave me was what made our communication break down.

When you care about someone, you want the world for them and will do anything for them. One thing many people do, even very empathetic people, is help someone the way we think they need help rather than how they actually want help. This isn't exclusive to bad times like my surgery news either. This can happen in completely unrelated good times too, like during sex when someone is really into something you're doing and you think that putting a finger up their butt is exactly what they want right now (pro tip: please don't surprise *anyone* with that out of nowhere). Everything you might be doing out of love in good times and bad, but it might be terribly misguided and totally off the mark. In my case, it caused a lot of emotional damage.

Now, I don't expect you to just know what to do at any given time. In fact, I'm not advocating for mind reading at all. People really suck at trying to be mind readers, and I don't advise trying to be one even if someone demands that you shouldn't have to ask what it is that they want because you should already know. That's either unrealistic or indicative that they don't feel like you're really listening to what they've told you in the past.

Not feeling listened to is definitely a massive cultural problem in close relationships I see over and over again. Typically, as you gain familiarity with someone or social norms of your surroundings, you might see patterns and have an idea of what to expect from them. You learn about what they like, dislike, and get downright pissed about. You see their quirks, frustrations, and favorite things in the world. We create social norms when several of these patterns become a common, collective expectation. You learn, remember, and implement these expectations and knowledge as you gain familiarity with them over time and exposure to that person or group.

Even then we can still suck at following these patterns. Logic is needed to follow patterns, but people are not always logical (just ask Spock, it annoys the shit out of him sometimes). We all feel emotions differently in the moment, and what we need when we're feeling these emotions changes from person to person and moment to moment. Our emotions are not one size fits all. While we know a lot about how we might feel in a situation, that doesn't mean that someone else would feel the exact same way.

Don't believe me? My friend Peter Benjamin from The Connection Institute taught me this exercise: try thinking of a flower right now. Picture everything you can about your flower. Where is it? What does it look like? How vibrant are the colors? Does your flower have a name? Once you have all of those things, write it down below. Draw it if you want to.

If there's someone else in the room or someone you can quickly message, tell them to picture a flower too. Don't let them tell you what theirs is yet. After you do, ask whomever you might have included in this exercise with you what their flower is. You might have had the same flower, or you might have had different ones. If you have no one to ask, you can compare it to my flower: the flower I'm picturing right now is a bright red hibiscus flower, still on the bush near some kind of tropical beach somewhere.

How different is your flower? It might be the same exact flower, but it might be completely different. It might be in a different place. It might be in a vase. It might be at a store. The complexities and variables for this can make it so that even if you have the same flower, it could be a different place, color, or location.

Try this with several people to get more variations and see how different they are. Tell them, "Picture a flower and don't tell me what it is yet. Picture where it is, the colors, what's around it. Okay, you got your flower? Awesome, my flower looks like this. What about yours?"

It's not like you don't know what a flower is, it's just that the word 'flower' is broad. It refers to a whole range of possibilities. The same is true for feelings. Sad and frustrated might not feel the same to me in a given situation as it feels for you. You could go through the same experiences as me, but you might feel and respond in a totally different way. For example, had you had the same experience as me, being questioned in my room by my mom – you might have withdrawn instead of lashed out like I did. Even when we see or are told that someone is feeling a certain way, we have our own idea of what that might feel like and, along with it, what kind of support someone wants in this situation. When you're wrong enough to hurt someone, you might inadvertently destroy trust.

Your emotions also have varying intensities, even on a day-to-day basis. To fall back on the flower metaphor again, the colors of your flower might be more vibrant or more muted depending on the day. For example, your version of "depressed" might feel more of a grey wilting lily today, but tomorrow it might feel like charred lily ashes that have no hope of repair. The next day, it might be a fully bloomed lily, just past its peak but still functioning very well. These types of descriptors are so important with understanding another person. If my mom had asked me about how upset I felt and I expressed it to her, she might have understood a little better how to react to my pain.

All of these checks for what it is someone else is feeling and how strong it is are all important so you can validate that feeling for them. If you can understand how someone feels, you can genuinely tell them that what they're feeling is legitimate, understandable, and accepted – and this is the most valuable thing we can give anyone. Validation doesn't mean that we're enabling them to act in bad ways as much as letting them feel the feeling that they have. Too many people (like my mom after I got the news about my knee) try to suppress these feelings in an effort to make us feel better, but when you try to suppress emotions, it doesn't necessarily make them go away. Instead, it often makes them rear their ugly heads later. How we feel isn't something that can be changed in a heartbeat just because someone tells us to stop feeling that way, so why the hell would we tell someone else to do that? Validating feelings gives strong emotions less power over the people you care about and allows them to eventually shrink to a manageable level.

Isn't seeing our loved ones manage their own emotions what we really want in the end? I sure as hell don't want to manage anyone else's emotions for them. That sounds exhausting as fuck. It's ironic that the more we try to solve other people's "problems" with how they feel or tell them what to do when emotions are intense, the less likely they are to listen to us. You've probably been on the receiving end of a lot of invalidation because you're isolated right now. You might have noticed that you're less likely to listen to your family or friends if they're being dicks about not letting you feel shitty for like five minutes while you have all your feelings.

We can't control how people support us without telling them how we most *want* to be supported. But you can begin to decide for yourself, just like I did, to ask for what you want. If you want to just feel your feelings with your friends instead of getting advice, you can ask for that without shame. If you want to hear none of this crap about thinking more positively about your situation, you can kindly tell your mom to let you just be miserable for five minutes while you get your shit together. If you want to just be seen for all that you're feeling and experiencing, you can ask for that too. Asking for what you want not only empowers you to receive what you need to move forward, but it empowers others around you to ask for what they want too when the roles are reversed.

This is actually a great place to apply the tools from the previous chapter. Asking someone what kind of box they want-- a soapbox, a tissue box, or a toolbox-- is a form of asking for what you want. The tissue box was what I needed from my mom, but she was giving me a toolbox immediately, and I wasn't ready to use that. Had she asked me what I wanted or asked if she could offer advice before she offered it unsolicited, this whole situation could have been avoided.

Chapter 6: Journal Prompt

Like the flower exercise, pick an emotion you're feeling right now. Describe it with more words, and include the volume on a scale of 1 to 10 for you right now.

Do you tend to minimize your own feelings more or do you tend to get feedback that feels like others are trying to minimize your feelings? Who's uncomfortable and minimizing in these situations?

People often say they are trying to help because they love you, but how they're helping isn't helpful. Responding to that from a place of love and caring is difficult but doable. Think about what you need right now that you're not receiving from your loved ones. Finish the sentence stem: "I love you too and want your help, and I need…"

Chapter 7: Mercury's In Retrograde As Long As You Don't Get off Your High Horse, Judgey McJudgePants

As someone with a hard science background, I have a long history of not taking anyone who is really into what I once considered "woo-woo crystals, hippy healing oils, and horoscope shit" seriously. Lavender essential oil smells good and is calming, but if someone told me it was going to heal my anxiety, I was going to talk to them less. My life has always felt tumultuous, but if someone told me it was because Mercury was in retrograde and I'm a Cancer with a Gemini rising and my moon in Aquarius, I was going to shut whatever shit they said next out of my ears. Oh, and I learned the hard way that crystal lovers don't like being told that their beloved amethysts likely involved as much exploitative child labor to get them as diamonds do. Not to mention anyone claiming to be a "healer" didn't seem to really do anything other than wave their hands around and stuff. These weird, unfounded beliefs made it hard for me to trust them.

The way many of these people speak didn't help me feel connected to them either. One word that has pissed me off the most was how many of them use the word "yummy." For some reason, there seems to be a correlation between people who are into woo-woo things and people using the word "yummy" unironically to describe a bunch of things that are not their food. This one time I went to a community event and some real woo-woo lady held her stomach and breathily reflected to the group, "This experience felt so *yummy*." My skin crawled, and I felt so much irrational animosity towards this probably really sweet woman when I heard her say this. I seriously considered not going back to that event ever again just because of this one instance. I hate hearing people call experiences "yummy" *that freaking much.*

It felt like the universe got a huge kick out of torturing me by putting "woo-woo crystals, hippy healing oils, and hororscope shit" people in front of me all the time so I could get even more pissed off and bitter with these people. So *of course,* many professional cuddlers are super into the woo-woo. Cuddling as a healing modality seems like a pure energy exchange on the surface, but most tend to forget complex hormone production happens when being touched that doesn't just involve oxytocin. And *of course,* many of them are into other woo-woo things and have crystals probably mined from child slaves. And *of course*, they give or receive Reiki which, for some reason, is more likely than professional cuddling to gain you respect while networking, even though most people don't even know what the hell it is. And of *fucking course,* they love describing some of their best cuddle sessions as "yummy." I don't know how I didn't see this coming, but I ended up being a sciency cuddle practitioner in a field full of overly holistic woo-woo people.

When I first started running into woo-woo people in my everyday life, I was the epitome of Judgey McJudgePants. I had my nose up in the air at the Karens that thought sitting barefoot surrounded by crystals and sprinkling essential oils on them was a valid alternative to seeing an actual doctor. I judged the hell out of their beliefs because how on earth could they be right? I couldn't take them seriously when the only links or "proof" they often gave me came from a website that was trying to sell me something. The problem came in when people that I trusted and made friends with years ago were showing their love and involvement in the woo-woo world. I mean, mindfulness is something based in science, which I value a lot – but the practice and the people it often attracts are not a far jump from Reiki, energy work, or the likes. I was really good at ignoring that woo-woo part of many friends who were close to me, especially if they didn't seem to ooze the woo-woo out of every pore on their body and with every word they spoke. My perspective on this topic started to change the day I made an unusual request to my surgeon about the pain meds I needed to take after getting my ACL operation. To my surprise, I suddenly found myself in a situation where energy healing actually became a solid alternative to my pain management.

· · ·

Just a week before my surgery, I was in the doctor's office going over last minute details for my surgery. As he told me what to expect in terms of pain management and medications post operation, I was forced to deliver a curveball that left my usually stoic surgeon looking suddenly worried.

"Addiction runs in my family," I said. "I can't risk getting addicted to these painkillers. What are my alternatives?"

He breathed in deep, held it for a moment, and shook his head with a sigh. "You will not be able to take the pain without these painkillers."

"I don't want to risk addiction," I snapped back. "That's pretty painful too."

The room went dead silent as he stared at me. I stared defiantly right back. I could hear the steady buzz from the monitor in the room as we continued our gaze for another long five seconds. When I saw he wasn't giving in, I could tell he wasn't lying about not being able to take the pain without painkillers. I was prepared to negotiate if I had to go on the painkillers. A family member that was on narcotics before warned me at what point it got harder for them to resist addictive tendencies. If I absolutely had to, I could handle a couple days on them but no more than that.

"If there is no other way, I need to get off of them as soon as possible after, and I need to know I'll have no chance of getting a refill."

He wiped his brow, trying to think of a solution. "Normally I write a prescription for ten days."

"That's too long," I interrupted. "I'm willing to be on them for five days max. What can we do after that?"

"There's nothing else I can prescribe," he insisted, "other than Tylenol and Advil. But those won't be enough at five days post-op."

I waived the concern off. "I have a high pain tolerance," I said. "I can spread out using the painkillers as needed until I run out."

He did not look convinced still, but I was headstrong on this. The odds weren't in my favor with drugs that are easy to get hooked on as it stands. I've experienced deep pain when I've seen other family members get addicted to alcohol and drugs. I was not ready to go down that route at the most vulnerable time of my life, and I wasn't going to make my loved ones try to pick up the pieces of my struggle.

The surgeon gave in. "In that case," he started, "I'll write you a non refillable prescription for half the pills I normally prescribe. Use them as needed and when you run out, switch to Tylenol and Advil."

"Thank you," I breathed out in relief. I didn't even realize I was holding my breath.

On my way out of the hospital my phone pinged. It was a text from my friend Alyssa. She suggested that if I felt I needed some energy healing that she'd be happy to help.

She runs a coaching practice and does energy work. I've known more about her coaching practice and stayed away from anything involving her energy work because it felt a little too out there for me to want to get involved in. She's one of very few people in that woo-woo world I felt good about getting close to because I knew her well before she went that route. Otherwise, I was skeptical and generally kept people like that *real* far away from me. I turned my screen off. No way will I ask her for that. It'll just be a waste of her time. But if she wants to come see me and use that as an excuse, who am I to stop her?

Four days after surgery, I took my last painkiller around 11:30am. Almost as if she was taking a queue, Alyssa texted me checking in on me just after I swallowed the last one. This is it. No more painkillers. I was going to have to deal with whatever pain I felt head-on now. Was I ready for it? I wasn't sure. I decided to ask her what her evening looked like. We planned for her to swing by my parents' house around 7pm that night.

Around 2pm that day, I started feeling the drugs wear off. It was dull at first and felt painful like it did when I was due to take another painkiller, so I was used to the feeling. But now it hit me that this pain wasn't going to go away like it had the past few days when I took my painkillers. Just like the surgeon said, Tylenol and Advil weren't going to cut it right now. Not only that, but my mind and emotions felt off. I knew I was reacting more than I usually did when I found myself pausing mid-sentence with my mom, her waiting for me to finish what I was saying. I felt my chest grow heavier. My head felt lighter. I began to feel incredibly, inexplicably hopeless. This hopelessness didn't stem from the pain, but it stemmed from a feeling of nothingness and despair. This felt like deep, inescapable depression, and within just a few seconds of these feelings starting, I began sobbing uncontrollably.

"What's wrong?" My mom shot her neck straight up, panicked and alert at my sudden change in mood.

What *was* going on? I was in pain, but not enough to be crying. I just felt suddenly very hopeless, like I needed something or someone to help me. Was this what withdrawals felt like? If so, no wonder people got addicted to drugs. Thank God I didn't get another prescription.

I went to lay down and take a late afternoon nap, but I couldn't. The pain was increasing and I was making pained moaning sounds without even realizing it. I tried propping my leg up higher and my mom got some ice for me. Despite my best efforts to get comfortable, I was still in pain. My mom squeezed the balls of my foot. That helped a little, but within five minutes, my knee was hurting again.

The hour before Alyssa was supposed to come by was excruciating slow. Instead of being too looped up out of my mind on drugs to feel anything like I had been the previous four days, I was writhing in pain in bed with my leg propped up on pillow and wrapped up in icy bandages. I struggled to keep it propped up on the pillows because the elevation was uncomfortable, but I needed to or it would be in even *more* pain. If this kept up, my poor parents would be up all night listening to me moan in pain every two minutes, and we had no surefire way to make it go away.

With my knee raging at me and nothing I could do to settle it down, I found myself feeling hopeful about Alyssa's Reiki. I didn't care anymore how out there it seemed or how little science there was supporting that it would help. If there was a potential that it could help me stop being in pain enough for me to be able to sleep and not keep everyone else up, screw science. If it didn't work, whatever. She wouldn't have to touch me, so I didn't think I had to worry about her making it any worse.

She finally arrived, and after a few pleasantries with my parents, she went straight to my mother's bedroom where she found me with the culprit propped up and straightened out on four puffy pillows.

"How are you feeling?" she asked me.

"I hate this," I moaned. "I can't do anything without it hurting right now."

"Well, if you're not doing anything you're not supposed to, that probably means it's mending itself right now," she said. I stopped and blinked at her. Of course she knew how bodies worked on some level. We did go to a high level private high school together. I realized that for some reason in an energy working role, I usually don't expect someone like that to be smart or believe in any science for some reason. That was pretty judgmental of me.

"Let me do some prep first, you don't have to do anything, just receive. Okay?"

Hearing Alyssa say that surprised me. I expected her to tell me something about my chakras being blocked or my energy fields being out of balance. Instead, she used language I was familiar with as a professional cuddler: receive. Yes, of course she'd speak to me how I'd want to be spoken to instead of waxing poetic about auras or energy fields. She knows me. She's my friend.

She pressed her hands together as if she was praying. She was quiet, but I decided not to watch her for this portion since she said I didn't need to do anything. Besides, it seemed that watching wasn't exactly helping the pain go away. I closed my eyes for a bit, trying to think of something else to focus on other than my knee pain and the fact that I finally agreed to this crazy hooplah of healing.

That's when I sensed something over my head. I opened my eyes to see her hands about two feet above me. She began slowly waving them from each side of my body, from my forehead down to my toes. I noticed that I felt different when her hands were near my hips, not my knees, but it wasn't necessarily pain. It just seemed heavy. She started making motions like pulling, plucking, and brushing in the air above me.

We made some idle chat as she made these various fluid motions over me. *Even though she is an energy worker, she is also my friend,* I thought. *I don't understand why she thought this was real, but I do value her, her opinions, and her own judgement. It's not like she's that gullible. Is there something I'm missing about all of this woo-woo, hippy healing shit? No, no way. This might seem very official right now, but there's no way that's why I don't feel any pain right now.*

...Wait, what happened to my pain? When I put my attention back on my knee, I realized that I stopped feeling the intense knee pains from earlier. I had been so relaxed and distracted from talking and watching Alyssa do energy healing hand waving that I didn't realize that the pain wasn't there anymore. I didn't even know the rest of my body was tense until I felt myself relaxing. My leg spasmed maybe two or three times while we were doing this, but overall I was feeling more of a warmth in my body than pain. My knee wasn't aching unbearably, and I began letting out a big, slow yawn every other sentence.

My eyes felt heavy. I was getting ready to sleep. "Alyssa, I'm not sure if I can keep awake now."

She silently clapped her hands in delight. "That's the goal! I'm a skilled energy worker." She started wiping her hands together as if she were washing her hands, creating a soft, satisfying brushing sound. "We're almost done today anyways." She started pressing her fingernails into her thumbs and rapidly flicked them into the air away from me almost like she was getting water droplets off her hands. Then she clapped her fingers together and continued a short closing ritual. At that point I was paying less attention to what she was doing and more attention to the fact that my knee's pain was dulled to a mere annoyance rather than a screeching pain. My eyelids started to stay closed a little longer with each time I blinked, despite it only being 8:30 on a Friday night.

I kept my eyes closed a few seconds longer when I heard the creaking on the wooden floor next to the bed and felt her reach for her belongings beside my bed. "I can do distance healing too, so if you're hurting like this again, just shoot me a text saying, 'Writhing in pain!' and I'll help you with stabilizing your energy field."

"Oh. Kay," I smiled loopily. "Thank you... so mu... muchhh, Alyssa." She laughed as I clearly couldn't stay awake any longer. I was drowsy. I saw her start to step out of the room and the last thing I remembered was hearing her talk to my mom about how she was a senior in high school when I was a junior before everything began fading around me and sounds got quieter, until they completely dissolved into a sleepy unconsciousness.

...

I woke up eleven hours later to Romeo meowing behind my mom's bedroom door. His habit was to meow my mom awake until she got up and fed her, but I was sleeping down in this bedroom now.

I checked my phone to see what time it was. I couldn't believe how well-rested I felt after what Alyssa had told me was her skilled energy healing. I noticed my head felt much clearer. I was better rested than I had been since my surgery. *I guess narcotics just knock you out, but it's not really restful sleep,* I thought. My mom came in a few minutes later to help me get my physical therapy started for the morning and she was surprised that I was asleep the whole time too.

That entire day, I felt more emotionally stable and clearer than I had since my surgery. Noah called me that Saturday morning to check in on me, unable to come down until the following weekend to see me. I was a little hesitant to tell him what happened because I worried he'd be judgemental about it, so I held back on it for now.

"You sound happier," he noted. *Do I?* I thought. *I guess I do.*

That afternoon, I had lunch and I noticed the pain in my knee coming back. I had taken Tylenol and Advil a few hours ago, so I couldn't take more for another two. As I kept my knee raised and remained motionless the pain started to come back no matter how I propped my knee up. More softness under it didn't help, and neither did slightly bending it.

She told me to just text her, I thought. But she was just here yesterday, so I felt really guilty asking her again. But hey, if this actually does work, the pain will go away, right? That's all I'm concerned about.

I grabbed my phone and I tapped out the message she told me to send her verbatim: "Writhing in pain!" I put the phone down and my knee was bothering me. I felt it ping a few minutes later. I'll see what I can do, she wrote back. Okay, so what the hell do I do now then? I picked up my phone, trying to distract myself with a mobile game to keep my mind off of things. Within a few minutes, I felt my stomach loosen like it was unraveling knots inside it. My knee's pains began to dull, and my eyes felt heavy. I put my phone down and adjusted the pillows behind me so I could lay down. I heard my phone buzz again, but I was too tired to answer it as I closed my eyes and let my mind fade to black again.

I woke up an hour later naturally. *What happened?* I thought. *I was having knee pain and – wait, my knee. It's feeling... okay?* I wouldn't go hop around on it, but it doesn't hurt just for existing at least. It felt a lot like it did that morning when I woke up.

I reached across the nightstand for my phone. I had a message from Alyssa about a minute or so after I had begun to feel more relaxed: "I'm stabilizing your energy field and that should ease things up a bit."

I didn't know what the hell stabilizing my energy field entailed, but I did know one thing: maybe this energy stuff isn't just for people that believe in all the pseudo-science. Maybe it's not all placebos and pretending like I thought. And maybe it's okay to trust people that do these things a little bit more and still have my own belief systems.

But I swear to God, if any one of them uses the word "yummy" to describe anything other than food, I'm still gonna have to keep my distance. That's one thing I just can't accept.

If you're human, you've judged someone before. Maybe you've judged them for having beliefs that conflict with yours. Maybe you've hid it behind concern for their well being or others' wellbeing. Maybe you're a bit harsher like me and you just felt like they were gullible, stupid people that got sold a bad bill of beliefs. Or maybe when someone does something, you judge their character and who they are as a person for doing it. We all judge other people in some form or another.

The fact that we judge each other is not necessarily a bad thing. In fact, I'd argue that judging people is how you can stay safe and protect yourself. Judging people can help you make decisions – from what neighborhood to live in to what grocery store to shop at. It's how you decide who you trust, from your best friend to the local cult followers that promise they'll never make you drink anything. It's how you decide who you pay to solve your problems, from your financial advisor to a life coach. It's how you figure out what information is legitimate, from academic journals to that conspiracy website your uncle likes so much that looks like it's stuck in the 90's (see what I did there? I judged that hypothetical site *hard*). We need to judge people and things in order to function on a day-to-day basis.

Most of the time, we judge ourselves just as much as we judge other people. In fact, this comes back to Chapter 1 where we took a hard look at how we see ourselves. When we judge others negatively, we also judge ourselves if we go along with them. Before my experience with Reiki with Alyssa, I identified as someone who trusts science and facts more than anything else, so I instinctively thought I could never be someone that would believe in "woo-woo crystals, hippy healing oils, and horoscope shit." But after the fact, I learned that there's tons of scientific evidence showing why some of these things work – evidence that is beyond just a placebo effect or a scammy sales page telling me it's true. I would have never realized this evidence existed if I had never gotten off my high horse to learn about it.

If there's a connection between judging ourselves and judging others, you bet your ass there's a connection between how close we can get to people when we judge them acutely. In astrology, when Mercury is in retrograde, it allegedly creates big problems with communication. It sometimes drudges up bad shit from past relationships in your current life. If you don't get off your high horse and evaluate your judgements, it'll feel like Mercury's always in retrograde. Think about it. If people are worried you'll be judging them, even silently, will they trust you with their deep thoughts about life? Will they judge you as well for not believing them? What feelings will come up for them when they don't feel trusted? How will they speak to you? All of this will probably be pretty shitty on both sides because neither of you will be willing to be 100% honest with each other.

This is why politics is often a dumpster fire of judgey party lines too – if you assume your opposing party of choice is an awful human being and is ruining the world with their heinous agenda, that will be fairly obvious in all your interactions with them and they'll treat you like shit too. Judging blocks us from being able to see who people really are and what their beliefs mean. You don't have to agree with them in order to not judge them, but you *do* have to understand what good intentions there are behind their beliefs.

It's time to dig into some hard-held beliefs you might be gripping onto for dear life. In the end, you might find that some of these are the same as they were at the beginning of these exercises. That's okay. As long as you have a stronger resolve and understanding to judge less and understand more while still having your beliefs, you've made way more progress with how you judge.

Chapter 7: Journal Prompt

Finish the following sentence with as many answers as you can (things, people, organizations, beliefs, etc.): I don't think I'll ever trust...

Look at the answers from the above exercise and pick one that stands out the most to you. Fill in the blank with that answer and answer the questions below.

I don't trust _____ because I see myself as...
I see _____ as conflicting with how I see myself because...

Now to ask thoughtful questions about what you don't trust. Try to avoid questions that have a yes/no answer (i.e Is energy healing fake?) and instead try an open-ended question (i.e what does energy healing do?). By asking open-ended questions that require a more in-depth answer, you'll uncover less biased hits on Google and you'll learn more about what it is you're curious about.

Before going to the internet to search for the answers, write down 3-5 open ended questions you can ask about this thing you don't trust.

Chapter 8: Stop Staying Awake At Night and Define Your Moral Compass

Growing up Catholic, I was immersed in my religion. I spent many Sunday mornings and weeknights at Confraternity of Christian Doctrine (you know, Sunday School for short, or CCD as most Catholics call it) in a windowless room full of children that didn't want to be there. I was the stern child, too serious to play along with my peers' giggling shenanigans when we were learning life-changing lessons about the Immaculate Conception. I was silent and focused during the hot days of summer Bible School, though once it came time to sing Bible School hymns, I was the loudest singing kid, belting out *This Little Light of Mine* and *O How I Love Jesus* at the top of my lungs. Luckily I was a good singer. This caught the attention of the church musicians, and I soon began sitting next to the altar during Mass to sing with ten other children in the youth group choir.

In the 5th grade, I started attending youth group nights. I loosened up a little and started to have fun, but my serious and quiet nature would turn back on whenever I sensed the adults wanted us to be quiet and serious for a second. My serious nature was the reason I wanted to be part of the Stations of the Cross. My mom sat through our performances depicting the 14 main events that happened the day Jesus was crucified. She watched children acting in the Stations of the Cross that didn't want to be doing this but still performed their part in a dull, unexcited monotone. I was the serious kid that happily and enthusiastically recited the only line I had in the stations. My mother later told me that it woke the entire audience up.

In high school, I went to a Catholic school. I was the one spearheading my parents' religious efforts by asking which Mass we were attending at the church that day. Some of the right people noticed that I often left my free period to kneel in the chapel praying by myself. I was specially invited to be a Peer Ministry Officer, even though they had already finalized their leaders for next year. I became the President of the Pro-Life March Committee, a group that organized the annual efforts for a trip to DC to protest the abortion laws. I did research on the arguments for pro-life and I spoke at visiting churches on how to address the arguments against pro-life. My parents supported me in these efforts, and I was on fire with the intention behind pro-life: we need to support everyone that exists and not let people die just because it would be convenient. At the time, I thought I knew what that meant.

Any opportunity for me to step up and make a difference in my religion, I took, and I easily became the poster child of the perfect religious youth. I didn't recognize that I could act independently within Catholicism until a couple of months after the Pro-Life March my senior year of high school. The first time I exercised that agency so acutely was when the head of the peer Ministry group on campus nominated me for an award in the diocese for my efforts on the pro-life movement. In it, she wrote something that I didn't do:

"Samantha campaigned and prayed outside of abortion clinics, urging pregnant patients going in to reconsider."

I did not do that and I did *not* sign up to do that. Not only that, but from my research on Pro-Life efforts, campaigning outside of abortion clinics trying to convince pregnant women about to get an abortion to change their minds was not an effective measure, and it was oftentimes way too late to intervene. I preferred to push prevention and education efforts well before making a decision about having an abortion was relevant to someone's life. That was why I focused on speaking at churches to youths that could spread these messages.

This line is either a mistake or a lie, I thought as I read the line over and over again. I wasn't comfortable with either of those, so I knew I had to bring it up to the Head of Peer Ministry. I carried the nomination over to her office and knocked on the department head's door. She invited me in, and I held the nomination so she could read it with me side by side. I pointed to the line about abortion clinic protesting.

"I'm not sure what you mean by this," I started, cautious and confused. "I didn't do this."

She relaxed her shoulders and waved her hand nonchalantly. "Oh, but you will." she said pretty matter-of-factly.

"Hold on," I said, a little alarmed. "I didn't commit to doing that."

She furrowed her brows, a little confused. "Yes you did," she told me. "When you became Pro-life president, that's what you signed up for."

My mind flashed back to when we "took office" of our commitments at a summer retreat. *Was that explicitly a commitment?* I thought. I scanned my memories of the new Peer Ministry Officer retreat, but nothing came up.

"No," I insisted. " I never said I would do that, that's not written anywhere on the commitment. Plus," I added, "I don't even know *how* to do that."

"I can give you everything you need to do it. Pro-lifers do this all the time, so it's easy." She responded quickly, yet still as nonchalantly and matter-of-factly.

She seemed to think I was bringing up the abortion protests to ask her how to do it, not to say I *won't* do it. I was convinced that going to abortion clinics was a good way to get a lot of bad press for the church, further discounting any valid messages we might have to help people. Images of standing with pro-life signs flashed in my eyes along with newspaper headlines: *Fanatical Catholic Schoolgirl Tells Pregnant Women at Abortion Clinic They're Killers.* I did *not* want to contribute to that kind of ammo for our efforts. Going to the Pro-Life March with thousands of people was one thing, but going to a clinic where the majority of the people don't want me there? That's a different story.

I finally just said it. "I don't want to do it."

"What?" She widened her eyes, incredulous that I actually said that to her. "Of course you do. You have to. You said you would." she said.

"What? No. I never said I would do that." This time I knew she was lying. I would remember if I specifically said I would do something like this.

What am I doing? I thought for a moment. It wasn't like me to speak up about something like this. Normally I would just do it and if I didn't feel good about it, I would remind myself I was doing it for the Lord. I would grin and bear it for however long I needed it to. What made this time worth fighting against?

"I'm not doing this. Take it out of the nomination." I insisted a little more forcefully.

The Head of Peer Ministry didn't like my newly found independence and hardened her eyes, glaring at me. "If you don't do this," she said, pointing a stiff finger at me and raising her voice, "I'll withdraw your nomination and you'll lose your title as President of the Pro-Life Committee… and I'll take you off the Peer Ministry Officer Board!"

Now she was *threatening* me? I felt my legs shaking, facing an authority figure I looked up to and trusted and realizing I was now the "bad kid" for not doing what she wanted me to do. I was backed in a corner and about to be scolded if I went through with this. Despite that fear, I was fighting because I thought she wasn't being fair, and my morals were strong about trying to be fair and truthful. I was terrified and convinced that this pushback meant I was in trouble.

Despite that, I dug into myself to try to find my sense of independent thinking, a weak muscle at that time. "I don't care," I said. "Take this out of the nomination because it's not true."

She ended up withdrawing her nomination, which drew attention from the principal. He found out about what happened and resubmitted the nomination himself without the part about going to abortion clinics. Even without committing to go to abortion clinics, I won the award and got invited to receive it from the bishop at a big Mass for multiple Catholic schools. The head of Peer Ministry didn't go through with taking me off the Peer Ministry Team when I won the award. In fact, she treated me as if that conversation never happened. But I remembered that conversation, and it left a bad taste in my mouth. Despite my serious and devoted exterior, this chain of events set off some serious soul-searching questions in me about my religious roots. I started taking an honest look at what kind of people were in my religion, and what it meant for me to be a part of it.

· · ·

After this unpleasant experience with my religion, I still identified as Catholic and a believer of God, but after I left my parents' house, I became resistant to practicing or being active in the church the way I was in my youth. I had a wonderful friend that kept me minimally connected to Catholicism in college, but as we graduated and saw each other less in our working lives, I began to fizzle out with my involvement. I began questioning the practices and the intentions behind some hard held beliefs. I began learning about other people's beliefs. It almost felt like it was a big secret to admit you were Catholic because other people my age had even *worse* associations with the religion than I did. I heard stories of LGBTQ friends being vilified, abusive pastors, and the very stories of abortion clinic protestors that I feared becoming. I identified less and less with my religion. I found myself losing sight of what it meant to be a person that believed in God. Even though I never stopped believing in God, I didn't know if being an active worshipper of God was a good idea. The landscape of painful stories about others' terrible experiences had me go to church a handful of times before leaving again.

When I was staying in my parents' house for those long two months, I was surrounded by signs of my Catholic roots. I would wake up in the morning and see the Serenity prayer on a card in my mom's mirror. I'd go to the bathroom and there would be a plastic cross on the wall. I'd sit in the lazy boy with my knee propped up, and my mom would be listening to Joel Osteen proliferate his sermons on TV.

It was only one morning when I was drinking coffee with my mom that I noticed how comfortable and easy it was for me to slip back into praying, making the sign of the cross with my hands, and drawing a cross on my forehead and heart. I felt a little embarrassed that these practices came so easily, despite not having practiced actively the way I had growing up in years.

I felt confused and guilty for straying away from practicing my religion. But at the same time, I didn't feel like I had pulled away from doing good. If anything, I found my own way to do good through many other practices outside of my faith. I found it through mindfulness practices, meditation, focusing on helping people more, and giving to others whenever I could. I had no doubt that these actions were influenced by God, but none of them were consciously done with God in mind. What did that mean for me and how I do things?

This question was what haunted me as I teetered between secular values and religious roots. I had the freedom to adapt and create fluid values within my secular values. That fluidity gave me the freedom to change as I learned, but it also meant I was constantly questioning my values. With religious values, I was free from ambiguity because we had a whole body of leaders that helped us figure out what was right or wrong. That doctrine we followed created the building blocks for my moral compass, but it never felt complete enough to *be* the moral compass. Neither of these solutions seemed like they had all the answers to me, and I sat with both options for a long time while isolated. How do I define what's right and wrong moving forward?

We all know the feeling of regret from thinking we didn't do the "right" thing. If you've ever stayed up late at night replaying a scenario you messed up in your head and what you should have done instead, you know what I mean. When given enough time with nothing else better to do, you're likely to start replaying not just the day-to-day moments where you made a mistake, but your life as a whole. If you're currently in isolation, you have a lot more time than usual to think about and evaluate the philosophical, existential and spiritual sides of yourself and how you've fucked up on meeting your overarching expectations. Even if you're generally proud of your moral compass, the fact that you have time now to think about your life decisions may have you second-guessing if you've made the Right Decision That's Better Than All Other Possible Decisions.

Social media doesn't help with this. We see so much pain and suffering online from individuals and long threads of arguments between people. Taglines from news articles need to be snappy and quick to read, so journalists name groups to oversimplify things and make people click on their articles. We get so much information in one sentence, but we get forced to make black and white decisions from these headlines alone when the world is anything but. By reacting constantly to our surroundings, we get more conflicting feelings, become judgemental about other people, and develop only shallow understandings of what actually happened. Anyone can have an opinion on social media, and anyone can respond and tell you why you're wrong. On social media, however, someone is *always* going to think you're wrong. Social media is an addicting game you cannot win.

When you question what your decisions mean about you, it's really easy to wonder if it means you don't belong to the group when most of the members believe something entirely different. I stood up to my Head of Peer Ministry because I had my own belief of taking action that's effective as a Catholic – not a Catholic that will do anything for my beliefs at all costs. But that didn't make me any less Catholic. In fact, my decision not to go along with her lie or protest in front of an abortion clinic didn't mean anything about my religious beliefs. What it meant was that I didn't believe that stopping abortion at all costs was worth losing tens, hundreds – possibly thousands – of followers that would benefit from our other beliefs. But as a teenager, I took my noncompliance to mean that maybe I wasn't a "real Catholic." With that conclusion, I decided that maybe I should leave Catholicism since I didn't agree with the whole group.

I'm not just talking to religious people or people with no connection to religion here either. If you're not religious in any sense at all and don't give a shit about what other religions think of you, you're not exempt from this line of questioning. If you grew up in a family that was actively practicing a religion even if you don't right now, you are likely in the habit of doing something that is tied to that religion, even if you're not a believer anymore. Repetitive habits from religion even if you're not an active practitioner of that religion anymore are easy to stay ingrained in our lives even in subtle ways. If you still catch yourself doing some of these simple small practices like making the sign of the cross or reciting a prayer, you're likely being judgemental and yet not severing your ties with what you're judging. This act of vilifying and yet following habit is contradictory and you're likely judging yourself constantly. Your first step as a nonreligious person is to go back a chapter and evaluate your Judgey McJudgepants self on how you view religious people (seriously, I've met super kind atheists, but some of you are real assholes to even remotely religious people).

One thing to note is that beliefs and spirituality are not static things because *you're* not static. You learn more, your beliefs change over time, you might "lose your way," you might go back to your roots, and you might take a stand for something you didn't know about before. Learning about other regions, lifestyles and philosophical beliefs may make your own beliefs stronger. We *need* people to have different beliefs from us so we don't become a crazy echo chamber of circle-jerking that never grows or learns. There is value in these organized beliefs and understanding their roots so that we can incorporate the principles into our lives in a way that's meaningful to us.

In fact, almost *any* organized group you're a part of provides value to more than just the people in the group. Contrary to popular belief, religion is not damaging. Religions that do harm for the sake of religious beliefs are damaging. The same can be said about community groups, secret organizations, rotary clubs, sports teams, political parties, and really anything else. Any people pulled into group think around a belief system that condones hurting people are the ones that actually fuck things up. We just make it out to mean that the group sucks ass as a whole if they do anything questionable. If we're associated with the group in question, this can really fuck up how we view ourselves and our own moral compasses.

The solution to our own moral questioning isn't to avoid being a part of any groups, nor is it to double down on being the most loyal member of the group without thinking. Rather, the solution is to reclaim your individualism WITHIN the group you're a part of. By reclaiming your individualism, you can be intentional about what you will and won't tolerate from the group. If the fundamental beliefs of an organization resonate with you, that's a good sign. If what they do to get there doesn't agree with you, then you might want to question if you can still stand by that.

Actively deciding what you won't stand behind is a really good thing if you're currently participating in or passively allowing something to happen in your group. It's good for you to be aware that this passive following is also a way of taking a stand. If you don't agree with what the group tells you to do, you are the best person to create the change you want in that group. A member inside of a group is more likely to guide big change to actually happen because they're calling on their close friends in the group to show up better too.

Being challenged on your beliefs and actions isn't a bad thing. Whether you're religious or you just try to be a good human, there is value from someone pointing out to you that maybe you need to consider adjusting. These moments get us out of mindlessly relying on groups to make decisions for us and put it back into our own hands to decide what is and isn't part of our individual moral compasses. Better yet, it's a good chance to be intentional and active in shaping your moral compass.

I want to make a distinction between groups where you disagree with how to do something and groups that are built on values that fundamentally hurt other people. There are groups whose purpose for existing is to claim they are better than other people and to make other people's lives outside the group miserable – or worse, to actively kill them. That is the textbook definition of a hate group, and those groups are vulnerable to spiraling into violence. With enough members that truly believe their lives would be better off if it weren't for another group of people, a group that was originally built on seemingly honorable beliefs can turn really toxic and cause real societal damage with fear-mongering and discrediting research or evidence. We have seen this time and time again with conspiracy theories, hate groups, white supremacist groups, and radical political parties.

It's not always easy to identify these hate groups, and the real pain in the ass is when a hate group points to an opposing organization and calls *them* a hate group, a fraud, or something else. With all this finger-pointing, how are we supposed to figure out which organizations are the real assholes here? Many hate groups will also hide behind a more noble-sounding motive for existing to seem more appealing and to continue their work. For example, doesn't "to teach and faithfully inculcate a high spiritual philosophy through an exalted ritualism" sound like a high spiritual calling kind of mission? Despite it sounding so noble, it's a direct quote from a pamphlet on the Ku Klux Klan's ideals and mission.

Other words to watch out for in many organizations like the Ku Klux Klan would be "maintain," "restore," "purification," "protect," and "preserve." These words are especially big red flags when they are referring to people, history, or ideals. If a group uses words like this to describe their ideals but the cornerstone of all their actions is centered around hurting other people (beyond just hurting their feelings), they are likely using their ideals as a shield. There's a good chance their "noble motive" is a nonexistent horseshit excuse so they can keep doing harm. Hate groups think they're doing good, but their moral compass includes pursuing some greater good at the direct expense of others. This might look like making it harder for people to make socioeconomic jumps, efforts to prevent or scare minority families in certain neighborhoods, rioting against peaceful protestors, or encouraging violence against specific groups of people.

While in isolation, it's really easy to dig into so much research on hate groups and their foundations. Going down an endless research pit for groups you're not a part of out of curiosity is useful yet *not productive for you particularly right now*. If anything, it will cause a distorted view of what the world is like by researching hate groups for extended periods of time unchecked. For the purposes of this chapter, I recommend examining your own involvement in these groups, if at all, for now. Otherwise, focus on what groups you are a part of and your own moral compass.

Chapter 8: Journal Prompt

What groups (religious, community, political, etc.) are you a part of? Circle the one that you most strongly identify with for your personal beliefs.

Look at the one you circled. What do you think they stand for? What do you see as the cornerstone of their existence from your experience? What are their values?

What don't you like about that group? What do some members or the group as a whole do or believe that you don't like? How does it conflict with what you believe in?

How can you show up for that part you don't like? Will you leave the group or take a stand against it? How can you make headway on that right now while you're not face to face with it?

What's something you can do right now to show up better? What do you want to do once you're done isolating yourself?

Conclusion: Resist the Urge to Make Up For Lost Time Socializing

I moved out of my parents' place and back into my apartment in April 2019. Even though I was close by after many months away, my friends were trying to respect my transition back as much as possible and wait for me to be ready to see them more often. I was okay with them giving me space because after months of a completely different life away from my friends and my typical day-to-day work and personal life, my usual extroverted self who needed people around me all the time was nowhere to be found. I had gotten used to solitude and didn't need to rely on others for my happiness, so I felt good being by myself. I did go to some house parties my friends threw every so often, but I wasn't as much of a social butterfly as I used to be. My friends were important, but my primary focus now that I was back to my apartment was to rebuild my business and rebuild my knee and leg strength. Socializing became an afterthought – something to worry about later.

It turned out waiting to worry about socializing later was a big fucking mistake and I should have prioritized it more than I did. Beyond my parents and Romeo (who still hated my guts but tolerated me at that point), I mostly talked with friends via text, video chat or phone calls. But being around people in person? It wasn't that I didn't like them – I enjoyed the connection, I just felt worn out really quickly. Sure, my business ended up booming with all the energy I put into it and my knee began to get really strong, but I hadn't socialized in person with people very much since I left in January. It wasn't until June when I began to really go out and see people more, and by that time I was awkward as all hell trying to engage in conversation. It felt like work to really engage with friends and even my boyfriend in person. I mostly just wanted to be to myself again. Yeah, my health and my business began stabilizing, but I couldn't handle more than a few minutes of being in a group for the life of me.

This became clearest when I went to my friend Kate's birthday dinner at a small restaurant in June 2019. That Saturday, I was in my bedroom playing on my phone. I hadn't left the house at all that day. I was tired, not that hungry, and not really wanting to be around people. I was perfectly happy being at home and not having to make conversation. Conversation felt hard and clunky to me these days, so I preferred my solitude when I wasn't working. Before my injury, it used to feel easy to jump into conversations seamlessly. Why didn't I want to do that all of a sudden? After all, I had gotten so good at keeping in contact in so many different ways when I was away from everyone.

Shouldn't I really want to be around everyone as much as possible now that I could be? The answer was no, apparently. As I watched the clock get closer and closer to 5:40, the time I'd need to leave to get to the birthday dinner on time, I did absolutely nothing. I was laying in my bed with my phone, playing games, with my hair still greasy from not washing it for two days, my clothes smelling a little dirty, and not a speck of deodorant on me whatsoever. As I watched the time pass by, I made not a single move to change anything about my current state.

5:40 rolled around and nothing changed. *Maybe I can at least change my clothes before I go?* I thought.

My Inner Critic seethed. *Can you please get your ass up now?* She snapped impatiently.

Trust me, I want to, but I don't have the energy, I replied groggily.

It wasn't like me to do this. I always tried to be on time so I could get the best seat, find the right cluster of friends to talk to, and be able to help direct the social sphere overall. This time, my mind ran through the things I would normally like doing and felt dread. I sank further into my bed, continuing to scroll on my phone, looking for an escape from the feeling of dread.

5:50. I considered cancelling. *Maybe I could make something up about something coming up at the last minute?* I thought. *No, who am I kidding, I'm a terrible liar. Why don't I want to go? Am I avoiding them?*

Finally at 6pm, I looked at the event page on Facebook and read that the birthday girl and other friends that live near her were running about a half hour late and called the restaurant to let them know. *Thank God. But even if I get myself ready and leave now, I'd still be arriving after all of them,* I thought. I felt guilty knowing that I'd be late even though I was doing nothing of any importance that would make me late.

6:05, I commented on the event post saying I'd be arriving just after the rest of the group, feeling weird about not giving an explanation. I put my phone down and sat up at the edge of my bed. I bent and straightened my bad knee. It wasn't at full strength yet, and I could feel its gentle pulls around the edges of my kneecap as I bent it. Staying still won't help it recover, I thought. I need to get up!

I lowered my feet onto the ground, feeling a cloud over my head and more light pulls from using my knee. Once again, I reconsidered cancelling. *Is it too late to change my mind?* I thought. I paused one last time before my resolve to go set in. *I'm going. It's her birthday.*

•••

I clicked my car remote to lock my green Toyota Corolla after I parked it on the busy street in Allston. My hair was still a little damp from a quick rinse in the shower, but I had brought a hairbrush with me and drove with the windows down in a sad attempt to dry my hair along the way. I was finishing braiding it to my side while I turned the corner to the Indian restaurant where I was meeting my friends. As I turned, I saw all of my friends spread across both sides of the restaurant. They had more or less taken over this tiny sitdown Indian restaurant.

I opened the door and searched for an empty seat. My friend Mike saw me first and everyone looked at me to greet me. I felt bad for interrupting their conversation, so I quietly murmured out some hellos and quickly scrunched myself into a seat to move attention away from me. For some reason, as soon as I sat down I felt like I had forgotten something important. I couldn't figure out what it was though. It was easy to simply sit down and give updates on what was going on in my life in less than two minutes – work and knee – and then stay silent as others talked about TV shows I didn't watch and trivial life things I found myself not caring about. I sipped my rum and Coke, keeping my mouth on the straw as someone else spoke so I had an excuse not to talk. I was trying to look like I was listening, but I kept finding myself not really listening. I wanted to, but after a few moments I'd mostly stare at people's faces blankly as if I were listening.

I felt really out of place. I could barely keep up with anyone and had little to contribute to the conversation. My head started feeling foggier and more out of sync by the minute. Normally I would have been effortlessly flowing into conversations boisterously. But today I felt run down and like every word someone said was hard to focus on. Finally, I remembered what I had forgotten. It wasn't a physical thing I needed to bring with me, but an ability I had left behind while I was recovering from my injury. I had forgotten how to have a casual conversation with all my friends at a table and feel good about it. As I realized this, I suddenly felt shame and like I was a bad friend.

I managed to make my way through the dinner with minimal conversation and a feeling of lethargy, which I fought to not let not show on my face. When it was time for us to go, some of my friends were figuring out rides back to their places. One friend, Mike, needed a ride back in the direction that I was going, so I offered him one. I almost didn't offer, but it seemed that most people were going in other directions so I wouldn't have to worry about a bunch of people suddenly piling in my car and having to deal with a group of people again. It would just be me and Mike, and I could handle that tonight.

Admittedly, Mike was probably the best person to have a drive back home alone with. I would often have conversations with Mike before I was injured and I felt like he really understood me. To put simply, Mike made a great Open Up To person. In that moment, Mike was the perfect person for me to open up to about how I was feeling about the evening.

I sighed as I plopped carefully into the driver's seat and started the ignition. "That was actually really hard for me to do just now," I confessed to Mike.

He nodded. Somehow, he seemed to know immediately what I was talking about. "Yeah, we haven't seen you in a long time," he started, "But I imagine it does take some adjusting to get back into being around people again."

I was surprised. I didn't expect him to pick up on that immediately, but I guess Mike was more aware of his surroundings than I gave him credit for. "It's not like I don't want to be a social butterfly," I bemoaned, pulling out of my parking space and into the busy street. "I really did… *want* to want to be there. "I care about all of you. It's just really hard for me to be fully present still."

Mike nodded. "I get that. It is really hard to see all of the people at once after not seeing them for so long."

Hearing Mike say that hit me suddenly. "Maybe that's why I've been wearing myself down like this," I thought. "I can't handle too many big group things yet."

"That would make sense," he agreed.

I noticed how I was beginning to feel a lot better and more energized just talking to Mike in my car. It wasn't just because Mike was a nice person to be around. After all, I was sitting right next to him in the Indian restaurant and didn't feel as good as I did sitting in the car with him chatting in the moment. This one-on-one conversation lifted this heavy cloud I felt over my head and had me feeling more human than I had in the past few weeks. I smiled to myself at this realization as I drove and listened to Mike the rest of the drive home.

After I dropped Mike off and he waved his goodbye, I reflected on why I might have felt weird. I don't think I felt weird just because I hadn't socialized in a while. No, if it was just a matter of needing people around, going to the restaurant would have been my solution. But the previous six months in recovery had been transformative for me. I wasn't the same person anymore.

I was just beginning to realize all these big changes I made in my life and applying them to my life in Boston. I had a better sense of my identity as a person and was learning to apply it in different parts of my life. I was prioritizing my body and wellbeing more while I worked. I was figuring out when, how and who I needed support from someone else. I learned how I communicate via text and phone calls and drew up different boundaries around those. I didn't accept other people minimizing my feelings and spoke out against it. My Inner Critic still grumbled from time to time, but I knew how to consciously evaluate her criticisms. Hell, I even tried energy healing and started to pay attention to my own judgey tendencies! With all of these things and more, I wasn't really the same person anymore. I needed to figure out how to bring my new life into my old social world, so of course I'd need to pump the breaks and ease my way back into my old social circles.

Even if you're normally the most extroverted person in the world, you're likely going to feel like an awkward hermit if you've been isolating yourself for months on end from others and then suddenly re-emerge into your social life. Being around people takes a lot of energy. If you've been forced to hermit, you've likely been using the energy you normally use to interact with people on yourself instead. If you're only isolating for a week or two, you might not feel your social skills go down too much. Longer than that, and you might forget how to be a social human being.

Many people's first instinct after not seeing people for so long is to dive right into as many social things as possible to make up for the lost time. Diving right into things the same exact way you did things prior to hermitting is a really good way to socially burn yourself out and question if you've lost who you are as a person. Especially if you've been going through this handbook and noticing an internal and external change in yourself, doing anything the same exact way you did before is going to feel weird and awkward. On top of feeling weird and awkward yourself, the people around you haven't seen you in a while and have to figure out how to reintegrate *you* into *their* social life. If you've changed significantly since they last saw you in the flesh, they have to figure out how to be around the new and improved you, not the version of you they remember you being. Simply put, you all need to figure out how you're going to fit into the group dynamic while you're trying to remember how to be a socially functional member of society.

Not knowing how to be a socially functional member of society after being by yourself for so long is normal and expected. Not knowing how to be a human in the social world doesn't make you less of a human and it doesn't mean something is wrong with you. It just means that you need to relearn how to socialize as the updated version of you. Diving right into your life as you knew it pre-hermitting days as soon as you're able to is the equivalent of healing a baby bird's wounds and then throwing it off a cliff to attempt to fly while it's peacefully asleep. That's a shitty thing to do to a poor baby bird, so don't do the same thing to yourself.

You might feel heavy and lethargic getting ready for bigger social events like I did. You might feel awkward conversing in person with people because you haven't in so long. You might even feel like you don't belong there, like I did at the restaurant. You might feel drained from feeling obligated to show up present and perky in other places too, like in the office, in your friend groups, with your family members, or anywhere else you'd encounter humans in the wild. These obligations and heavy lifting to socialize won't feel good at first.

Not feeling good at first doesn't mean you shouldn't socialize with people though! In fact, I encourage you to prioritize the important things in your life and still find time to socialize a little bit with other people *somehow*. This might mean saying no to certain outings that you just mentally can't handle. Most good friends won't fault you for easing back into socializing since you've already been away for so long, and as for those who do, you can simply tell them that you're still taking care of yourself. Your health, especially your mental and emotional wellbeing, needs *way* more nurturing during this transition back to society than ever. If anyone tries to peer pressure you to come back into the Fold of Very Big Group Social Shenanigans before you're ready, you may need to have a one-on-one conversation with them about how not being there right now doesn't mean you care about them any less.

One awkward social dynamic you might worry about happening is if you don't go to events when people invite you, they'll stop inviting you even when you are ready. This can easily be combated by simply telling them that you appreciate the invites and you want the invites in the future, but you're not able to go to them quite yet. This intentional and conscious decision to say you want to go in the future can be powerful for the people inviting you to not assume anything about you. Verbalizing your intentions and wants in this way also helps calm your own fears that saying no means that you'll be excluded in the future. You do want to go! You just don't have the emotional energy to be with all your loved ones yet. Remember, you've been hermitting for a while and re-learning how to socialize takes practice. You're not going to be on your A game when you are trying to track multiple conversations at once in person. Eventually, you may want to go from one-on-one coffee meetups to making dinner with a few close friends. You might want to play games with some friends. You might want to go watch a movie but skip going to dinner afterwards until you're ready for that. This isn't a perfect science, but the more you can treat socializing like exercising, the more likely you'll be able to build your social skills back up to where you want to be again – possibly even better than they were before.

I encourage you to do the journal prompts below even if you're at the end of this book and still isolating. This will help you get some perspective on what to expect and how to intentionally build back up your social life.

Conclusion: Journal Prompt

First, how long have you been hermitting so far? If you're still isolating, how long do you think you'll have to keep hermitting? If you're out of isolation, how long have you been back out and socializing?

Think of some activities that you'd enjoy doing with one to two other people. Name specific people if you can think of them, but focus on the activities first. Add to the examples I provide below

Go for a walk

Cook together

Think of some activities that you'd enjoy doing with two or three other people. Name specific people if you can think of them, but focus on the activities first. Add to the examples I provide below

Go to a bar

Go hiking

Now think of some activities that you really want to be able to do that involve 5 or more people. These are activities you might seldom do at first (if at all), but as you get comfortable with smaller groups you can do more of these. Add to the examples I provide below

Go to a concert

Have a dinner party

Any and all of these might tire you out because you're not used to doing them so often. Like a muscle, you need to rest so you can recover and build up your social muscles. What will you do to rejuvenate yourself after socializing?

Lastly, it's really easy to forget the time you had hermitting actually had some happy times. What don't you want to forget even as you reintegrate back into life as you knew if before?

Holy Sugar, You've Read the Whole Book!

Thank you for reading. I hope you come out of your isolation as good if not better than when you went into isolation. I hope you've become happier while you've been hermitting and that this book made you think and re-evaluate your life and how you show up. I can't wait to hear about what you've done to make your life better as a result.

As a shameless plug, as I referenced in this book, I do professional cuddling. One way I've found to help people readjust to their social life after isolating is to find a space where they can simply be themselves. Whether it's being one of the CORE4, receiving in-person connecting cuddles, or to simply have virtual cuddling calls with me, I invite you to consider working with me directly in your reintegration to society. You can learn more and start the process at **snugglewithsam.com.**

About The Author

Samantha Varnerin graduated from Worcester Polytechnic Institute in 2013 with a Bachelor of Science in Civil Engineering. She traded her life of construction sites and schedules in 2017 to be a full-time professional cuddler instead with her personal practice, Snuggle with Sam. Through cuddling, she discovered that her mission in life is to make sure no one ever feels alone on their journey. While weaving through the worlds of neurotypical and neurodiverse people, she loves learning about new people's life experiences and strives to get a stranger's life story in 30 minutes or less upon meeting them at a party. She is also a certified facilitator through The Connection Institute and a Certifield Cuddlist.

Made in the USA
Middletown, DE
18 May 2023

30300980R00078